Philosophy, Art, and Religion

At a time when religion and science are thought to be at loggerheads, art is widely hailed as religion's natural spiritual ally. *Philosophy, Art, and Religion* investigates the extent to which this is true. It charts the way in which modern conceptions of "Art" often marginalize the sacred arts, construing choral and instrumental music, painting and iconography, poetry, drama, and architecture as "applied" arts that necessarily fall short of the ideal of "art for art's sake." Drawing on both history of art and philosophical aesthetics, Graham sets out the historical context in which the arts came to free themselves from religious patronage, in order to conceptualize the cultural context in which religious art currently finds itself. The book then relocates religious art within the aesthetics of everyday life. Subsequent chapters systematically explore each of the sacred arts, using a wide range of illustrative examples to uncover the ways in which artworks can illuminate religious faith, and religious content can lend artworks a deeper dimension.

Before taking up his post at Princeton Theological Seminary, Gordon Graham taught philosophy at the University of St. Andrews, where he was also founding Director of the University Music Centre, and at the University of Aberdeen where he was Regius Professor of Moral Philosophy. The author of many essays on a wide range of philosophical topics relating to art, ethics, politics, and religion, his books include *Philosophy of the Arts* (third edition, 2005), *The Re-enchantment of the World* (2007) and *Wittgenstein and Natural Religion* (2014). He has been Sheffer Visiting Professor of Religion at Colorado College, Stanton Lecturer in Philosophy and Religion at the University of Cambridge, and an Adjunct Professor of Sacred Music at Westminster Choir College.

Cambridge Studies in Religion, Philosophy, and Society

Series Editors

Paul Moser, *Loyola University Chicago*
Chad Meister, *Bethel College*

This is a series of interdisciplinary texts devoted to major-level courses in religion, philosophy, and related fields. It includes original, current, and wide-spanning contributions by leading scholars from various disciplines that (a) focus on the central academic topics in religion and philosophy, (b) are seminal and up to date regarding recent developments in scholarship on the various key topics, and (c) incorporate, with needed precision and depth, the major differing perspectives and backgrounds – the central voices on the major religions and the religious, philosophical, and sociological viewpoints that cover the intellectual landscape today. Cambridge Studies in Religion, Philosophy, and Society is a direct response to this recent and widespread interest and need.

Recent Books in the Series

Roger Trigg
Religious Diversity: Philosophical and Political Dimensions

John Cottingham
Philosophy of Religion: Towards a More Humane Approach

William J. Wainwright
Reason, Revelation, and Devotion: Inference and Argument in Religion

Philosophy, Art, and Religion

Understanding Faith and Creativity

GORDON GRAHAM

Princeton Theological Seminary

CAMBRIDGE
UNIVERSITY PRESS

University Printing House, Cambridge CB2 8BS, United Kingdom

One Liberty Plaza, 20th Floor, New York, NY 10006, USA

477 Williamstown Road, Port Melbourne, VIC 3207, Australia

4843/24, 2nd Floor, Ansari Road, Daryaganj, Delhi - 110002, India

79 Anson Road, #06-04/06, Singapore 079906

Cambridge University Press is part of the University of Cambridge.

It furthers the University's mission by disseminating knowledge in the pursuit of
education, learning and research at the highest international levels of excellence.

www.cambridge.org
Information on this title: www.cambridge.org/9781107132221
DOI: 10.1017/9781316450789

First published 2017

Printed in the United States of America by Sheridan Books, Inc.

A catalogue record for this publication is available from the British Library

Library of Congress Cataloging-in-Publication data
Names: Graham, Gordon, 1949 July 15– author.
Title: Philosophy, art, and religion : understanding faith and creativity /
Gordon Graham, Princeton Theological Seminary.
Description: New York : Cambridge University Press, 2017. |
Includes bibliographical references and index.
Identifiers: LCCN 2017020800 | ISBN 9781107132221 (alk. paper)
Subjects: LCSH: Arts and religion. | Art and philosophy.
Classification: LCC NX180.R4 G73   2017 | DDC 201/.67 – dc23
LC record available at https://lccn.loc.gov/2017020800

ISBN 978-1-107-13222-1 Hardback
ISBN 978-1-107-58477-8 Paperback

Dedicated with gratitude to the presidents, faculty, and students of Princeton Theological Seminary during my tenure there from 2006 to 2018.

Contents

Preface

This book is the culmination of a decade offering courses in philosophical aesthetics to divinity students. Before my appointment (in 2006) to a newly established position in philosophy and the arts at Princeton Theological Seminary, I had taught aesthetics over many years in the philosophy departments of two largely secular universities. Covering an appropriate curriculum in these contexts allowed limited reference to religious art, but it certainly did not require it. Books and papers were few in number, and in fact the subject of the relationship between art and religion was infrequently and only lightly touched upon in the growing number of guides and handbooks to aesthetics that were coming out from academic presses. Even the college text I myself published (*Philosophy of the Arts*, 3rd revised edition 2005) made only fleeting references to religious art. As a consequence, the move to teaching aesthetics in a divinity school presented both a challenge and an opportunity.

The challenge was to engage with second degree students who generally had little or no background in philosophy and no knowledge of the traditional topics of aesthetics, while at the same time convincing them that philosophy in the Anglo-American analytical tradition could have interesting things to say about the subjects that interested them most – namely, Christian faith and practice. In addition, there was the challenge of ensuring that it was indeed *philosophical* aesthetics to which they were being introduced, and not the burgeoning area of *theological* aesthetics that was developing at the same time. This meant largely ignoring the rapidly growing literature in theological aesthetics, even though any alternative literature I could call on for reading lists that would be directly relevant to the topics of my courses was very limited indeed. At the same time, the other side of this challenge was a corresponding opportunity to uncover new connections between philosophy, art, and religion, and to preserve philosophy's distinctive mode of thought with its emphasis on conceptual clarity, dialectical exchange, and argumentative cogency while avoiding the level of abstraction that often leads philosophy to leave the substantial content of art and religion behind.

I had already begun to think about the issue for the Stanton Lectures in Philosophy and Religion that I gave at the University of Cambridge in 2004 (subsequently published in 2007 as *The Re-enchantment of the World: Art versus Religion*), but it took some years of experimentation to find the right way of combining a serious education in philosophical aesthetics with a deep interest in religion. Part of the solution lay in focussing less on general concepts such as beauty, aesthetic experience, and aesthetic judgment (or "taste"), and more on the philosophy of the arts, especially those arts that have had a prominent place in the history of religion, chiefly music, visual art, and architecture. But a larger part of the solution, it turned out, was to engage a little more than analytical philosophy customarily does in the cultural history and anthropology of art and religion, to think about art in the context of religion as a distinctively human *practice*, and to explore and reflect on both major and minor religious artworks and artists.

The result might be called "empirically enriched philosophy," a phrase that some anthropologists have used to describe their subject.[1] But the difference with anthropology, as I see it, is that philosophy has the additional aim of attempting to resolve the problems and paradoxes that arise when we try to combine certain concepts and ideas that are central to the arts – music and emotion, depiction and resemblance, truth and fiction, beauty and usefulness, for instance. It also has an essentially normative element – the desire to determine the human significance of the phenomena it seeks to understand. It is interested not only in the character of the human practices that constitute art and religion, but in why and to what extent they matter.[2]

---

[1] I owe the expression to Professor Tim Ingold, a former colleague at the University of Aberdeen. He illuminatingly sets out his distinctive conception of relational-ecological-developmental anthropology in the introduction to *The Perception of the Environment: Essays in Livelihood, Dwelling and Skill* (London and New York: Routledge, 2000), though he does not use the expression there.

[2] My own conception of the kind of understanding philosophy seeks is articulated at length in 'Philosophy, Knowledge and Understanding' in *Making Sense of the World: New Essays in the Philosophy of Understanding*. Ed. Stephen R. Grimm. (New York: Oxford University Press, in press).

Most of the examples I drew on in class were taken from the Christian religion, a natural consequence of the fact that I was teaching in a Christian seminary. But I tried, as did many of my students, not to lose sight of the fact that it was the philosophy of art and religion, not one particular religion, that we were primarily there to study and to teach. In this book, accordingly, the range of examples is much wider, and though I am most familiar with Christian music, painting, literature, and architecture in the Western art tradition, I have also drawn, so far as my knowledge will allow, on Judaism, Islam, and the religions of the East.

My position in Princeton proved to have some additional benefits. Its relative novelty gave rise to conferences, exhibitions, and other events that included artists, musicians, theologians, and educators among the participants. In these contexts also there was the challenge of showing that philosophy has something distinctively interesting to say, as well as something to learn from other rich disciplines. A number of invitations to lecture elsewhere gave me occasions to organize my thoughts in a more sustained way. One especially valuable stimulus was the invitation to teach for a couple of years as an adjunct professor on the Masters degree in sacred music at Westminster Choir College in Princeton.

This book is an attempt to capitalize on all this. The literature relevant to philosophy, art, and religion is more extensive than it was, but not very much more so, and my hope is that this book will constitute both a contribution and a stimulus to its expansion. It traverses some of the same ground as *The Re-enchantment of the World*, but in a sufficiently different way, I trust, to make it worth reading as well. It also makes a special effort to assume as little familiarity with philosophy on the part of the reader as possible. Chapters 2 and 4 contain substantially reworked material that first appeared in the journals *Faith and Philosophy* and *Theology Today*. Chapter 5 builds on a lecture I was invited to give at the University of Nice.

I owe a great debt to Princeton Seminary. Having created the Henry Luce III Chair in Philosophy and the Arts, the faculty left me completely free to realize its ambitions in whatever way I thought best. But I owe an even greater debt to several generations of students whose questions and comments, both in class and outside it, constantly stimulated me to think more imaginatively and productively than I would otherwise have done.

Art, Religion, and the Aesthetics of Everyday Life

Reweaving the Rainbow

For several decades, the cultural world of Europe and North America has been marked, dominated, it might be said, by the "clash" between religion and science. A recurrent theme of much discussion in newspapers, radio, television, and online is whether the rise of science inevitably means the decline of religion. As the use of "rise" and "decline" suggests, these apparently related phenomena are easily viewed as just two sides of one coin. Science, it is commonly held, at both the level of theoretical explanation and of practical manipulation, has proved to be far more successful at doing what in the past the Christian religion (and religion more generally perhaps) claimed to be able to do. Modern science, this view of the matter contends, offers far better explanations of the physical world, the biological world, and the social world than the theological stories about creation, providence, and miracles we find in the Bible. Still more importantly, by producing technologies that give human beings much greater control over their lives and prospects than prayers and rituals ever did, science has fundamentally altered the human condition. We don't need God (or the gods) anymore, because thanks to technology we can protect ourselves from the elements, literally dispel the terrors of the night (with artificial light), and, by using modern methods of transportation, eliminate most of the dangers historically associated with travel. Medical science, too, has played an important part in this change, rendering redundant archaic spells and petitionary prayers for healing. Of course, these age-old practices persist. In reality, however, or so this new scientific enlightenment claims, the superiority of medicine is acknowledged even by people who cannot quite bring themselves to let go of their religious beliefs. Modern "believers" still offer up prayers of healing certainly, but this does not lead them to abandon drugs, physicians, and medical research, in which, in truth, they actually place far greater hope.

If this way of seeing things is correct, then it does make the rise of science/decline of religion idea very plausible. Given that religion and science are competitors, huge scientific advances such as there have undoubtedly been, on two fronts – the explanatory and the practical – must mean that religion inevitably, and ever more rapidly, is forced to beat a retreat. And yet, even in highly developed societies it has not died out completely. No modern state is entirely secularized, but in many religion has been pushed out of the public sphere and into the sphere of privatized spirituality.

The line of thought just expounded has many adherents, and in some quarters would be taken to be stating the obvious. Yet in other quarters it remains an open question and a matter of serious debate whether religion and science are indeed rivals. Claims about the triumph of science and the end of religion were especially prominent at the turn of the twenty-first century, but it is important to remember that such claims have a long history. They stretch back to the eighteenth century at least, and even to the seventeenth. With the appearance of Darwin's *Origin of Species* in 1857, the "conflict" between science and religion received fresh stimulus, and claims about the triumph of science and the death of religion generated widespread debate for most of the remaining nineteenth century. After some time, the debate receded, though it never quite disappeared, perhaps. At any rate it has gained great attention once again. Some scientists have written books that sell millions of copies, often with the aim of finally destroying "the God delusion."[1] Some philosophers have joined enthusiastically in "breaking the spell"[2] of religion, by which, they allege, large numbers of people are still held captive. Meantime, theologians, other philosophers, and a few scientists have responded, often no less vigorously, either with the aim of restoring religion's scientific credibility,[3] or showing that the two are not rivals at all.[4]

In this way an old debate has been revived, though it has not proved any more conclusive than previously. Part of the reason for its inconclusiveness is that the practical "triumph" of science is not as straightforward

---

[1] Richard Dawkins, *The God Delusion*, (London: Bantam Press, 2006)

[2] Daniel Dennett, *Breaking the Spell: Religion as a Natural Phenomenon*, (New York: Viking, 2006)

[3] John C. Lennox, *God's Undertaker: Has Science Buried God?* (London: Lion Hudson, 2009); Alister E. McGrath, *Why God Won't Go Away*, (London: Nelson, 2011)

[4] Stephen J. Gould, *Rocks of Ages*, (New York: Random House, 1999)

as many of its protagonists suggest. Modern technology has at best been a *qualified* source of good. If science has given us penicillin, it has also given us the atomic bomb, and while truly extraordinary advances in telecommunications have been immensely valuable, the technology of the internet and the smart phone has also aided criminality, been a stimulus to vindictive abuse, and encouraged child pornography. It has also been widely used for "sharing" information that is essentially trivial. Of course, enthusiasts for modern technology can argue with some plausibility that these "downsides" are more than offset by the immense social and commercial benefits that have been made possible.

Perhaps this is true, though difficult to estimate with any degree of confidence. Still, the value of technology does not settle the issue about science and religion. It is easy to find powerful voices on the other side of the theoretical debate also. Philosophers have presented compelling arguments that constitute serious challenges to the explanatory superiority of science, and powerful analyses that expose the "atheist delusions"[5] upon which a lot of scientific triumphalism rests. Even professedly atheistical philosophers do not always sign up to the unqualified success of science. Some of the most distinguished have denied that natural science adequately explains the phenomena of "mind and cosmos,"[6] while others argue that if we consider the issues between science and religion more closely, we will find that the most prominent warriors in the battle are mistaken about "where the conflict really lies."[7]

The existence of opposition to the pretensions of science is not surprising. As was observed earlier, though the debate was renewed with special energy at the turn of the twenty-first century, it is both an old and a recurring one. While its most recent occurrence has undoubtedly witnessed new voices and some fresh angles, it is also true that claims which sound novel to new audiences are often re-articulations of long established positions. To describe them in this way is not to dismiss them, of course. There is both demand for and value in, new ways of restating old views. At the same time, while genuinely innovative thought on these matters can never be ruled out, in times past when the debate has subsided, it has generally been because scientists, philosophers, and theologians find themselves repeatedly treading exceptionally well-known ground,

[5] David Bentley Hart, *Atheist Delusions* (New Haven: Yale University Press, 2009)

[6] Thomas Nagel, *Mind and Cosmos* (Oxford and New York: Oxford University Press, 2012)

[7] Alvin Plantinga, *Where the Conflict Really Lies* (Oxford and New York: Oxford University Press, 2011)

occupying the same positions and rehearsing the same arguments. Once this happens, a kind of exhaustion sets in, and attention moves elsewhere.

One direction in which those who have tired of the science/religion debate might move, is to consider religion's relationship to another important aspect of modern culture – art. Here, it is common to suppose, defenders of religion should find themselves on more congenial ground. If the intellectual "battle" between science and religion has inevitably cast them as cultural rivals, art and religion, by contrast, are widely held to be cultural allies. The histories of art and religion, especially in Western European culture, are intertwined and their aspirations are mutually supportive. Or so it is quite widely thought. The agreeable expectation, consequently, is that investigating their relationship holds out the prospect of a conversation rather than a contest.

This hope is undoubtedly rooted in fact. Religion and art are often in sympathy with each other. It is not only religious believers who worry about the cultural dominance of science and the conception of reality that the success of scientific ways of thinking appears to validate. Poets, painters, and composers also often lament the materialism this success brings with it. As they see it, when human beings subscribe wholeheartedly to a scientific conception of reality, the result is a kind of spiritual impoverishment – a "disenchantment of the world,"[8] to use Max Weber's famous phrase. By objectifying and quantifying everything, the artistic mind alleges, science robs human experience of its humanity.

This lament is not new either. It was given a memorable expression, possibly its most memorable, in the early nineteenth century by the English poet John Keats (1795–1821). What we call "science," Keats called "natural philosophy," a more familiar name at the time. He writes:

> Do not all charms fly
> At the mere touch of cold philosophy?
> There was an awful rainbow once in heaven:
> We know her woof, her texture; she is given
> in the dull catalogue of common things.
> Philosophy will clip an angel's wings,
> Conquer all mysteries by rule and line,
> Empty the haunted air, and gnomed mine –
> Unweave a rainbow.[9]

---

[8] Max Weber, 'Science as a Vocation' in *From Max Weber: Essays in Sociology*, edited and introduction by H. H. Gerth and C. Wright Mills (London: Routledge, 1948)

[9] John Keats, *Lamia*

But why should science have the effect of "disenchanting the world" and "unweaving the rainbow"? The answer implied by Keats's poem is that while the scientific method of inquiry has proved a successful method of investigation in many respects, it requires us to re-conceive the *whole* of reality, the reality of our own minds as well as our bodies, in purely mechanical terms. That is to say, science, (or "natural philosophy") understands reality as a vast complex of interlocking, measureable and quantifiable systems. The explanatory power and the impoverishing effect of scientific ways of thinking have the very same source. The sciences of astronomy, physics, biology, and psychology uniquely help us to understand and master the worlds of nature and the human mind, but only by interpreting them as systems whose internal relations can be exhaustively captured within the formulation of quantifiable causal laws.

If this is true, it seems that the underlying vision of the scientific world view, broadly speaking, is "deterministic." This makes it indifferent to human beings as *subjects*. By becoming an object for investigation and manipulation, humanity is importantly separated from its subjectivity, its self-conscious awareness. Science presents nature to us both as a source of knowledge, and as a means to satisfying the desires that our biology generates. Viewed in this way, though, the world in which we find ourselves ceases to be an *environment*, which is to say, a place to be at home, to love, and to delight in. It becomes, rather, a vast machine of which we are just one functioning part. Keats's lines, then, give compelling voice to this lament: while a scientific vision of reality may be highly effective in conquering "by rule and line," it simultaneously eliminates the "feel" of experience, and thereby our delight in the mystery of existence. That, after all, is the point; science aims to explain *everything*,[10] and with the aid of explanation, bring as much as possible under the subjugation of human needs and desires.

The belief that there is no aspect of reality that the natural sciences cannot capture and master, is not itself a discovery of natural science. It is a metaphysical view about the power and value of a particular form of investigation and explanation. For that reason, it is more accurately referred to as "scientism." But even the most ardent proponents of scientism will agree that their aspirations in this regard are far from complete. They readily accept that there is much we still do not know, and much that we cannot yet control. They take the undeniable fact of scientific *progress*,

---

[10] The great aspiration of modern physics is often described, in fact, as a "theory of everything" or TOE.

however, to both reflect its real accomplishments and to rationally ground their faith in its steady advance toward this goal.

Another way of putting this same idea is to say that, scientifically conceived, the world either *excludes* anything we might properly call "spiritual," or *re-interprets* the spiritual as a by-product of material causes. The mournful wind, the glittering stars, the form of the rose, the pattern in a snowflake can all be explained in terms of physics and chemistry. We no longer need to appeal to divine design or spiritual energy of any kind. Those who want to destroy the God delusion and break its spell in the name of science, expressly acknowledge this. Indeed, they insist upon it. But the poet's complaint is that while their intention is to exclude divine or supernatural spirits and anything that could be regarded as "spooky," the full effect of their explanations is to eliminate the human spirit as well. Where, the poetic mind asks, do love, and beauty, and courage, determination, imagination, and playfulness, fit in to this interconnected complex of deterministic systems? It seems that in so far as these are "explained" by the physical and biological sciences, they are explained *away*. Romantic love becomes a hormonal reaction to external stimulus whose value and importance lie chiefly in the part it has to play in reproduction. Similarly, love of children is explained as a built-in biological response with proven evolutionary advantages for the species. Imagination is the faculty by which we generate useful survival strategies. And so on. At one level these hypotheses *about* human life may be true. The trouble is they do not seem to leave any room for *living* it.

To express the point succinctly: the understanding of the world that science offers us is, quite literally, dispiriting. There can be no doubt that science has proved hugely successful on an explanatory level, and has produced an enormous number of valuable technologies. Only "creationists" and "Luddites" of various kinds could deny this. Nevertheless, the scientific vision of reality is not one that human beings can live by. It tells us how things work. It tells us how they can be manipulated to deliver the basic needs we find we have – nurture, food, shelter, sex, freedom from pain, and so on. The problem is that while knowing how things work will give us the power to manipulate them, it will not tell us what it would be good to use this power to do. Nor will it tell us whether, and why, the things we want to do truly *matter*. Neither knowledge nor power can in themselves make the life of a human being *mean* anything. Once we are struck by this dimension of existence, we need to look elsewhere.

These are real limitations to scientism. Someone who has no inclination to question the validity of modern science, and who happily makes use of all the devices modern technology has given us, may nevertheless intelligibly raise questions of meaning and significance. Such a person wants the world of physical and biological processes to be infused with a value other than that of interesting or useful information. This desire is not in any way "anti-scientific." On the contrary, it is often highly successful scientists who are most inclined to put the truth and the usefulness of their theories in second place, and express their greatest enthusiasm for the beauty and the wonder that their studies reveal to them. At the level of the beliefs of practising scientists, there is no very strong correlation with atheism, and many will say, in fact, that a powerful sense of wonder lies at the heart of the attraction science holds for them. Their inclination in this regard accords with Keats's implicit assertion that the human spirit is not fed by fitting experience into some formula of "rule and line." We want, and need to be able, to see the world as something more than a mechanism, however large, intricate or complex. Only then can it be the sort of world in which it is possible for us to lead purposeful, valuable and meaningful lives.

Of course, Keats's poetry, however compelling, falls short of a demonstration of the assertion implicit within it. As far as the debate between science and its critics is concerned, there is plainly much more to be said. The brief articulation offered here simply states what many have claimed – that a purely scientific conception of the world is radically deficient from a human point of view. It does not show this affirmation to be true. What it does do, however, is provide a context within which we can think about the relationship between art and religion. Can both be regarded as importantly spiritualizing alternatives to the materialistic conception of the world that the success of science seems to require us to endorse? Might they together serve to counter, or at any rate check, the cultural dominance that "science" currently seems to enjoy? In other words, are art and religion natural *allies* in the task of combatting the "disenchantment" that Keats feared? And will their ability to do so be maximized, if they find ways to act in concert? This, certainly, is the supposition behind some hugely successful collaborations between the two – art exhibitions, musical events, poetry festivals. It also serves to explain the rapidly rising number of books and periodicals that have art and religion as their theme, as well as the creation of new organizations and institutions whose purpose is to bring art and religion closer together.

Yet, just as it is a mistake to assume that science and religion are necessarily *rivals*, so it would be a mistake to assume that art and religion are inevitably *allies*. While both casts of mind and experience may share reservations about the consequences of an exclusively scientific view of the world, that is not sufficient in itself to show them to occupy important common ground. It does not even show that they are mutually support-ive. Art and religion could be found to have importantly divergent ways of addressing the deficiencies of science, in which case there may in the end be an element of rivalry here too. It is at any rate a possibility to be borne in mind while their relationship is investigated more closely. One essential preliminary to such an investigation is to see what the history of their relationship has been.

Religion and the Birth of "Art"

In his earliest work – *The Birth of Tragedy out of the Spirit of Music* – Friedrich Nietzsche (1844–1900) claims that we can find the origins of both music and drama in the religious rituals of ancient Greece. It may be questioned whether the historical thesis that Nietzsche advances is strictly correct, but the real purpose of his book does not actually lie in tracing the history of art to its origins. He means, rather, to highlight the difference between two ways of thinking about art (a subject we will return to in the next section). There is something right about his opening contention, however. It is easy to identify a link that goes back to the ancient world connecting religion and what we think of as the arts – music, painting, sculpture, architecture, story, poetry, drama, and dance. This is true across many different cultures. The Vedic Hymns of Hinduism, for instance, are believed to be the longest surviving oral tradition in the world, dating from the present day back to the time of Homer – roughly 1000 BCE. The Hebrew Scriptures, some of which are possibly even older than this, explicitly refer to the use of music and dance in acts of worship. Archi-tectural construction, in the form of the building and re-building of the Temple in Jerusalem, also figures centrally in the development of the Jew-ish religion. The oldest of all are the ancient cave paintings in Lascaux in south west France. These may be as much as 17,000 years old, and some experts suggest there is reason to think that they had a religious purpose and were connected with ritual dance and the worship of the stars.

    The most evident connection between religion and art, however, and the one which will provide much of the material for this book, is to be found in Christianity's relationship to European, or Western, art in all its manifestations. The earliest Christians were Jews, of course, and contin-ued using the hymns and psalms with which they were already familiar. Soon they were adding new material of their own. Paul's *Letter to the*

Philippians includes what was probably an early Christian hymn. Soon, too, Christians began to paint pictures with religious subjects, thereby deviating from the Jewish prohibition on religious painting (a prohibition that Muslims also adopted some centuries later). At the beginning they met for worship, prayer, and Bible reading in houses, and though we do not know very much about the origins of Christian architecture, we do know that the practice of constructing and decorating buildings as dedicated sacred spaces was an early one. Statuary, poetry, and drama, which had served religious and quasi-religious purposes in the ancient world were also called upon to serve the interests and purposes of Christians, and when Christianity became the official religion of the Roman Empire under Constantine, the Church first joined and then superseded the State as the principal patron of the arts.

This close connection lasted a long time. Over many centuries, painting, sculpture, architecture, music, and poetry were taken to new heights in virtue of their connection with religious life and the worship of the Christian Church. As a result, the world now possesses a vast collection of religious buildings, paintings, statues, and frescoes, devotional poems and sacred music, an artistic inheritance that includes many works that have been heralded as among the greatest masterpieces of all time. Not all these masterpieces were produced for the Church, and many are not explicitly Christian. Alongside markedly religious works, history has left us indefinitely many compositions, books, poems, pictures, plays, and more recently movies, that have broadly "spiritual" themes, especially if we include under the label "spiritual," moral and psychological subjects. These include such masterpieces as the plays of William Shakespeare in which expressly Christian concepts are almost wholly absent. Explicitly religious motifs make a very limited appearance, and yet the profundity of his greatest plays undoubtedly derives from the fact that they deal with enduring aspects of the human spirit – the outworking of ambition, corruption, redemption, and forgiveness in the lives and fates of the characters and events the plays depict. Shakespeare's themes are in a very broad sense religious, even if he does not deal with them in an obviously theological way.

We may justly conclude, then, that the use of music, literary art, painting, statuary, architecture, and poetry for religious and more broadly spiritual purposes is very ancient. At the same time, the use and development of the arts for other communal purposes – social solidarity, political authority, imperial aggrandizement, military conquest – has also been an important part of their historical development. The world possesses a large number of works of art whose origins and purposes are not religious, or even spiritual in the widest sense, but political – castles and palaces, royal portraits, landscapes, military music, and patriotic poetry, for instance. These alternative purposes may be said to have accelerated greatly in the Renaissance, that extended period in the fifteenth and sixteenth centuries when medieval other-worldliness receded and European culture found new inspiration in the humanism of the ancient worlds of Greece and Rome. Classical styles, myths and legends, as well as surviving fragments of sculpture, provided artists of every kind with new subjects of a largely non-religious kind. Meantime, increasing economic prosperity generated a burgeoning market for the work of painters, architects, dramatists, and musicians, paid for by patrons who had made large sums of money in trade and manufacture.

Ironically, perhaps, developments within the Christian Church aided this change. While preference for "silence" unadorned by poetry or music as the mode best suited to apprehension and contemplation of the divine was a recurrent tendency in the church both East and West,[11] it was the sixteenth century Protestant Reformers, in their anxiety to purify the Church of what they regarded as pagan cultural accretions, who encouraged the destruction of paintings, statues, stained glass windows, altar pieces, and so on. All these, they believed, had resulted in idolatry. The power and attractiveness of beautiful objects had deflected ordinary believers from properly spiritual worship – the worship of God – and become objects of worship in themselves. In this respect the Reformers were echoing the same anxiety as the iconoclasts of the eighth century who had attacked the use of icons in the worship of the Eastern Church. Combined with the Protestant emphasis on the sole authority of the Bible, the Protestant Reformers effectively came to share, and to endorse, the ancient Jewish prohibition of "graven images" inscribed in the second of the Ten Commandments delivered to Moses on Sinai. In many cases, in fact, prohibition was extended beyond images. Protestant suspicion fell on other arts, and expressed itself in, for instance, the replacement of ornate polyphonic settings of the Latin Mass with far simpler styles of church music, and the construction of much plainer buildings in which to meet for worship.

While some branches of the church underwent a significant artistic austerity, neither the practice of art making, nor the creative impulses of artists went away, of course, even in Protestant countries. They simply

---

[11] See Diarmaid MacCulloch, *Silence: A Christian History* (London: Allen Lane, 2013)

found alternative avenues of expression. An especially notable example is to be found in Holland and the Low Countries. Long home to many famous painters, by the seventeenth century religious art was increasingly discouraged by the now largely Protestant Dutch Republic. The consequence was not the cessation of painting, however, but the development of still life, landscapes, and portraits with secular subjects as valued alternatives. Moreover, so successful was this new development that, despite being deprived of religious patronage, the seventeenth century eventually came to be regarded as the "Golden Age" of Dutch art.

The humanist Renaissance and the Protestant Reformation, then, were both historical influences that did much to turn European art, and especially painting, away from the service of religion. This was not an immediate or even rapid change, but one that spanned more than two centuries. It was relatively late in this history that a distinctive concept of "Art" as we now think of it emerged, when the labels "fine arts" and "mechanical arts" ceased to be current, the first being replaced by the singular "Art" and the second by the concept of "Design." Along with this new concept of "Art" came the related concept of "the aesthetic." This is an invention of eighteenth century Europe that can be dated very precisely in fact. Its invention both reflected and reinforced the belief that works of art did not need to serve the purposes of patrons, religious, political, or otherwise. They could, and should, be accorded value in their own right; that Art should be contemplated *for Art's sake*. In turn this belief reflected an important cultural change. The arts began to acquire a significant measure of cultural autonomy. Having hitherto been largely employed in the service of politics and religion, the idea of "Art" as something that not only could, but *ought* to be promoted and engaged in for its own sake arose.

Striking evidence of this new way of thinking is to be found in the emergence of artistic institutions. The Royal Academy of Fine Arts Antwerp was founded in 1663. This was the first of its kind in Europe, but widely replicated over the next 150 years, a period during which many of the most subsequently prestigious academies were founded. These included the Académie Royale des Beaux-Arts in Brussels (1711), and the Royal Academy in London (1768). The establishment of academies of music followed soon after, beginning with the foundation of the Royal Swedish Academy of Music in 1771. It was in this period too that dedicated art museums, concert halls, and opera houses came into existence. They are now such a thoroughly familiar part of most urban landscapes, as well as objects of both civic and national pride, it is important to remember that it is just two centuries or so since people first thought it necessary to create special places exclusively devoted to the arts. Some were adaptations of existing buildings; the Louvre Museum, for instance, which opened in 1793, was created out of the Louvre Palace which had stood in the center of Paris since the twelfth century. Others were housed in specially constructed buildings that were themselves artistic commissions; the Hanover Square Rooms in London, where the music of Handel and Mozart was performed, were purpose built in 1775 and had space for an audience of 900. Unlike churches, palaces and parliaments that had long employed the arts and architecture as a means by which to enhance and enrich the pursuit of religious and political aims and ideals, these new institutions called forth magnificent buildings for the celebration and advancement of the arts themselves.

It is precisely at this point that we first see the potential for art ceasing to be the ally of religion, and becoming something of a rival instead. Having lost the patronage of a large part of the Church, the arts had to look for other sources of material support, and found them, not only in alternative patronage, but in a commercial market for artistic production. Painters, composers, writers, sculptors, dramatists, and architects discovered that increasing leisure and prosperity meant many more people were interested in their work, and most importantly, willing to pay for it. The result was that in the nineteenth century artists were generally held in high social esteem, were often quite wealthy and gained the status of national celebrities. In France Delacroix the painter, in Italy Verdi the composer, in Germany Goethe the writer, in England Tennyson the poet, and in Scandinavia Ibsen the playwright and Thorvaldsen the sculptor, are all especially clear instances of this. Together this list of names encompasses celebrated and famous contributors to almost all the major arts. The image of the artist starving in a garret because he (or she) has sacrificed everything to art owes more to nineteenth century Romanticism than to historical reality. A talented artist was far more likely to be socially successful.

It was as "Art" rose in cultural importance, that rivalry between art and religion first became an important possibility. Some evidence of this can be found in Friedrich Schleiermacher's celebrated *Speeches to the Cultured Despisers of Religion*, published in 1799. While Schleiermacher himself saw a natural affinity between art and religion (though he admitted that he could not say exactly where the affinity lay), the "cultured despisers" he meant to address were members of a prosperous social class whose admiration for art was almost directly proportional to their distaste for religion. As the nineteenth century wore on, and Christianity confronted further important challenges from both historical criticism and evolutionary biology, it seemed to some that art would finally displace religion. Friedrich Nietzsche, probably Christianity's most implacable critic, summarized the thought in this way.

Art raises its head where religions decline. It takes over a number of feelings and moods produced by religion, clasps them to its heart, and then itself becomes deeper, more soulful, so that it is able to communicate exaltation and enthusiasm where it could not do before .... [G]rowing enlightenment has shaken the dogmas of religion and generated a thorough mistrust of it; therefore feeling, forced out of the religious sphere by enlightenment, throws itself into art.[12]

Nietzsche's prediction was fulfilled only to a modest degree. While religion in general, and the Christian religion in particular, did undergo significant decline in some parts of Europe, contrary to his expectation, and that of many others, it did not die out, and experienced something of a revival even in surprising places. In France, for instance, the *Basilica of Sacré Coeur*, which now dominates the Paris skyline, was under construction at the very time Nietzsche wrote these words. Still, it is true that in some of its forms, art in the first decades of the twentieth century came to see itself as a spiritual alternative to traditional religion, and a preferable alternative because it offered a kind of spirituality that was unencumbered by outdated metaphysics.[13] At the same time, although this rivalry was historically influential, and philosophically important, the relationship between religion and art fell far short of the hostile opposition that the rivalry between religion and science often provoked. Indeed, even if "Art" more grandly conceived found autonomous purposes and institutions that enabled it to claim a distinctive spiritual status, Christians, both individually and collectively, went on deploying all the arts for religious ends. Sacred music continued to be composed and commissioned, paintings continued to have religious subjects, devotional poetry and novels with religious themes continued to be written. The construction of religious buildings was widespread and continued to attract some of the best architects.

This fact greatly complicates the issue of their relationship. In the eighteenth century and thereafter, it can be agreed, "Art" ceased to be

---

[12] Friedrich Nietzsche, *Human, All Too Human*, trans. Marion Faber and Stephen Lehmann (London: Penguin Books, 1878, 2004) §150
[13] See Jacques Barzun, *The Use and Abuse of Art* (Princeton: Princeton University Press, 1974) and Gordon Graham, *The Re-enchantment of the World: Art versus Religion* (Oxford: Oxford University Press, 2007)

dependent on the Church as a patron and created a world of its own – known to philosophers as "the artworld." Since religion lay at the origins of this world, however, the inherited art on display in museums, academies of art, concert halls, and so on, inevitably included a great many religious subjects. Furthermore, influential artists, composers, and novelists still wanted to engage with such subjects. It is possible, on the basis of such facts as these, simply to dismiss Nietzsche's prediction, and declare that, while artists did other things as well, the relationship between art and religion continued much as it had been. This response, though, overlooks a wholly new and indisputable factor – the artworld. Could it be that art's continuing relationship with religion was simply residual, the lingering effect of a long history that was likely to vanish eventually? Certainly, in the course of the twentieth century expressly "religious" painting and literature became just one, rather small and not very significant part of a far larger world. The autonomy and social prestige of the arts undoubtedly changed the context within which religious art was to be made and received. Just how big a difference did this make? *Contra* Nietzsche, autonomous art did not have the effect of replacing religion. A more interesting question is whether its effect was transformative, so that even in religious art the beauty of holiness effectively gave way to the holiness of beauty. This is a topic to be returned to, but for the moment it is important to observe that it was not only art's relationship to religion that these important developments changed.

"High Art" and "Folk Art"; "Art" and "Design"

Let us suppose it to be true that the eighteenth century witnessed what Larry Shiner has called "The Invention of Art."[14] Whatever way we interpret this contention, it cannot alter the obvious fact that the artistic practices underlying this invention – painting, acting, music making, storytelling, and so on – had existed for centuries, since before recorded history even. What then does it mean to say that "Art" was an historically dateable *invention*? One widely accepted answer to this question is this. Painting, music making, storytelling were not new in the eighteenth century. But it was not until that period that they finally began to realize their full potential. Freed from the constraining contexts within which they had previously been obliged to operate, the arts at last came into

[14] Larry Shiner, *The Invention of Art: A Cultural History* (Chicago: University of Chicago Press, 2001)

their own. The arts, we might say, gave birth to "Art." This account of the matter is one that Nicholas Wolterstorff has called "the grand narrative of art in the modern world."[15] Notwithstanding its widespread acceptance, and the powerful influence this "grand narrative" has exercised in both philosophical aesthetics and art history, Wolterstorff argues that it is false, and must be abandoned if we are to gain a proper understanding of the role of the arts in human life. His claim is one to be considered further, but first it is necessary to say something about how this "grand narrative" has shaped the way we think about the role of the arts in society.

The historical developments that we have briefly considered gave rise to two important distinctions in terms of which aesthetic interest came to be understood. On the one hand, artistic artefacts – pictures, songs, and so on – were increasingly categorized as either "high" art or "folk" art. Secondly, the activity of art making was similarly divided into "Art" and "Design." Together these distinctions constituted a framework of thought that gained very great currency. This framework is still employed widely, and relatively uncritically. "Folk" art can now be found more frequently in art museums, than previously and "Design" often appears alongside "Art" in the advertised curriculum of colleges of art. Even so, these distinctions are still being drawn.

The first of them may be said to be a product, as well a reflection, of the emergence of the institutions and organizations that came to constitute the "artworld." "High" art was the art of the art museum, the royal academy, the concert hall, the opera house, and the theater, while "folk" art remained within the province of everyday life. This distinction had another important dimension. Folk art continued to rely on traditional material – folk songs, folk stories, country dances, and so on, whose origins were obscure – and to be primarily a source of popular entertainment. "High" art, on the other hand, was increasingly identified with intentionally produced *new* works by reputable artists. Such works were to be valued exclusively as objects of "aesthetic" contemplation. By raising it up from the level of mere entertainment, this emphasis on aesthetic contemplation gave high art a different evaluative status. Folk art was still valuable, but only as a pastime. High art was on a different plane. It was to be valued as the inspired creation and attentive contemplation of beauty for its own sake. Thus the enjoyable familiarity of folk singing, for

[15] Nicholas Wolterstorff, *Art Rethought: The Social Practices of Art* (Oxford: Oxford University Press, 2015)

instance, though an exercise in musical art, fell into a different category to the ambitious compositions and sophisticated performances of the concert hall.

The art of dancing provides a specially striking example of the way that this distinction could alter social practice and cultural prestige. Before the eighteenth century, dancing was a common pastime amongst all classes. Of course it could be done well or badly, elegantly or inelegantly, but the form of engagement was active participation. Those who attended a ball but did not dance, played cards instead; country dances were communal, and organized for good, bad, and mediocre dancers. Then ballet came into existence. In contrast to the dances of both barn and ballroom, this was "artistic" dancing, and required a degree of talent possessed by relatively few people, and a dedication to training possible for only a small number of committed "professionals" sustained by dancing "schools." Consequently, for the vast majority of people, the form of engagement with this new kind of dance could not be participation. It had to be observation. Some danced while others watched, thus becoming spectators rather than dancers. In ballet, dancing found a form that both needed and warranted an audience. Indeed, as if to make the point, ballet was distinguished sharply from mere "dancing," and even came to be described explicitly as "painting in movement." To describe it in this way signalled that, as with great paintings, dancing was an art form that could offer spectators the pleasure of aesthetic contemplation.

Something similar can be seen to have happened with music. Composers demanded ever more technical virtuosity from their players, so that once again exceptional talents and intensive training came to be required. The effect was that in the concert hall *making* music was delegated to a few, and *listening to* music became the norm for the majority. "Art music," as it sometimes came to be called, construed music as "painting in sound," and offered the audience an art object – the composition – to be listened to with same close attention one might devote to a painting, and with the expectation of a similar aesthetic reward. As a consequence, over time composers rather than players came to be regarded as the principal "artists" in music, the artistry of the player being reconceived as a *means* rather than an *end* – namely, the means by which the aesthetic goals of the composer could be realized. This alteration took time, of course. Bach, Handel, Mozart, and Beethoven were all both imaginative composers and highly accomplished players, admired for their musical virtuosity as much as for their highly original compositions. A century later, however, it was possible for a great composer such as Tchaikovsky to concentrate on composition at a relatively early stage in his studies, and to leave musical virtuosity to others.

Over much the same period, the second distinction – between "Art" and "Design" – also came to be widely employed. In this case the difference was not between the homely and the high flown. Art was seen as essentially autonomous, an end in itself. The value of Design, by contrast, lay in the *usefulness* of the things it produced, their practical convenience or saleability. Designers, however elegant or ingenious their designs, have to serve, and satisfy, *exogenous* purposes. The objects they produce – clothing, furniture, tableware, interior décor, and so on – must be useful and not just beautiful. Fashion design cannot simply be about the aesthetic contemplation of beauty. Clothes are made to be worn and they must serve that function well. Practical, not aesthetic, considerations determine the necessary dimensions of chairs and beds. Knives, forks, cups, and wine glasses can be beautifully attractive, but they are not there simply to be looked at; they must facilitate eating and drinking. By contrast, artists properly so-called (so this distinction implies) are not constrained in this way. In Immanuel Kant's phrase, they can submit themselves to the "free play of the imagination," guided solely by a purely *endogenous* goal – to produce that which can be contemplated with aesthetic delight.

Over the course of two centuries, the gap in cultural status between "high" art and "folk" art grew even wider. High art came to be regarded as having a value and significance that folk art simply does not have. Perhaps this estimation was as much the outcome of social and economic differences as of philosophical ideas and conceptions. High art often traded on tastes and preferences that only the wealthy could afford to indulge. But this was not the only, or even the principal reason. With its newfound status, art attracted many people of great talent and dedication, as well as a new set of patrons. Consequently, works of art were produced whose sophistication and complexity did actually warrant sustained attention and study. Accordingly, new academic disciplines grew up around them – literary criticism, art history, musicology, architectural theory, and so on – and these in turn elevated the arts still further.

The twentieth century witnessed something of a countermovement, a self-conscious attempt to raise the status of folk art by according it a much greater degree of attention. As a result, the term "high" art has generally been abandoned as indicative of an unacceptable snobbery. Nevertheless, even this attempt can itself be seen to reflect the extent to which the contrast between "Art" and "folk art" has become entrenched. Those who want to challenge the pretensions and counter the dominance of "high" art, generally seek to do so by bringing the paintings and drawings of folk artists into the art museum, or incorporating folk tunes in the music of the concert hall, or producing illustrated and annotated editions of folk tales. In all these ways, of course, they imply that folk art cannot be left to languish in its natural home. In order to be given the same status as "Art" it must be put on display in the dedicated spaces of the artworld.

The second important distinction – between art and design – grew equally marked over the eighteenth and nineteenth centuries, though without the same degree of evaluative difference. When the "fine" arts became simply "Art," design initially inherited the more lowly status of the old "mechanical" arts. But then, as machine manufacture of fabrics and other household goods became more widespread, design found reason to assert its own special value over against the purely "mechanical." The "arts and crafts" movement of the late nineteenth and early twentieth centuries, for instance, did not set itself to claim the same status as "Art," but to affirm the value of skilled and imaginative design, initially in the context of interior décor, over against cheap manufacture. Its protest was not against exclusion from the art gallery, but against the poor aesthetic quality of mass produced goods. Across the years that followed, it proved possible for fabric and fashion designers, furniture makers, interior decorators, jewellers, and silversmiths to become famous, wealthy, and held in high regard. Here too, however, more recent attempts by the artworld to give craft its due have an irony about them. Many art museums and galleries now include extensive collections, and sometimes special exhibitions of furniture, fabrics and silverware. Famously, "modern" art galleries have made a point of displaying "readymades" which is to say manufactured objects, a practice that grew out of Marcel Duchamp's celebrated (if initially whimsical) submission of a porcelain urinal to an art exhibition in 1917. The unhappy implication of all such attempts to "display" the products of design, however, is that these things attain the same status as art only when they are removed from the practical sphere for which they were intended, and made objects of purely aesthetic contemplation. But something has gone deeply wrong, when useful objects are denied any use.[16]

The ease with which we now use the contrasts between high art (or simply Art), folk art and design, is evidence that the "grand narrative" identified by Wolterstorff has been profoundly influential. Indeed, even

---

[16] The relationship between the aesthetic and the pragmatic is a subject to be returned to in Chapter 5.

those who want to break free of such dichotomies can still find themselves operating within the very same framework of thought, and this, it
seems safe to say, shows that the distinctions we have been discussing are
here to stay in one form or another. This does not mean that the "grand
narrative" cannot be challenged, but what most needs to be challenged
is a philosophically more significant, and much more contentious aspect
of it. This is its claim that the concept of "Art" which emerged in the
eighteenth century brings to its fullest realization something that is only
partially present in folk art and design. The underlying idea is that art
making of even the simplest kind gives expression to a deep-seated human
impulse. This is the common element that we find at work across the folk
arts of traditional stories, song, and dances. With the advent of academies
of art and music, the building of museums and concert halls, the theater,
and so on, the impulse that drives all art underwent a transformation in
accordance with which the arts were elevated from every day pastime to
aesthetic experience, a transformation, in some minds, that raised them
from the mundane to the spiritual.

It is this claim about the "apotheosis" of art – its elevation to a higher
plane – that is key to the "grand narrative" that Wolterstorff aims to challenge in *Art Rethought*. Since the course of history cannot be rewound,
it seems pointless simply to lament what has come to pass. But what we
take "history" to be and to signify is a matter of interpretative understanding as well as fact. Wolterstorff's principal contention is that the "grand
narrative" that so often and so easily shapes our understanding of the
history of art, actually *distorts* our understanding, and continues to mislead us deeply about the true nature and value of art as a social practice.
It does so because, out of the many purposes art making can have, this
account of art's development elevates just one – contemplative aesthetic
experience – and makes this one possibility the defining purpose of art as
a whole.

"Art for Art's sake" and the Vita Contemplativa

Though we are thoroughly familiar with the practice of looking and
listening attentively to deliberately created works of art, it is important
to be reminded that it was not always so. During the liturgical service
for which J. S. Bach composed the *St. Matthew Passion*, now considered
one of the greatest musical works of all time, people arrived and left as
their circumstances required, and generally paid closer attention to the
sermon than to the music. Shakespearean plays, to take a different kind of

masterpiece, were interspersed with swordfights and clowns, and played to audiences that bought food from hawkers shouting out their wares. Even for later and less rowdy audiences, "aesthetic contemplation" was not the order of the day. Mozart complained to his father that people in the polite circles for whom he was invited (and paid) to play the piano, often talked while he did so. Nearly 200 years after Shakespeare, when the Louvre in Paris first opened as an art museum, notices had to be placed on the walls to tell the public to look at the pictures rather than use the long halls for games of *boules*. In short, people took a long time to learn the practice of giving works of art their undivided attention. Once they had mastered this practice, though, what was it they expected, or were promised, in return? The century that invented "Art" also provided the answer to this question. Contemplating works of art in and for themselves would result in a very special kind of experience – aesthetic experience.

The greatest and most influential philosophical exponent of this idea was Immanuel Kant. Kant was the author of three philosophical *Critiques*. The first, the *Critique of Pure Reason* aimed to lay out the rational foundations of genuine knowledge. The second, the *Critique of Practical Reason*, aimed to show how reason operates quite differently, though no less rigorously, in deliberating about courses of action. A third critique, the *Critique of Judgment*, proved to be necessary, however, because judgments of beauty, Kant thought, are neither theoretical nor deliberative. When we judge something beautiful, we are not stating a fact about it, and while we do mean to commend it to others, what we commend is not that they take some consequent course of action – buying it, for instance – but simply that they attentively contemplate it. Judgments of beauty are not directed at thinking or at acting, but at looking, listening, and touching as aesthetic experiences.

As these few sentences suggest, in his third *Critique*, Kant was more concerned with beauty than with art, and though his text dwells at some length on the subject of artistic genius,[17] he holds that natural objects can be judged beautiful no less than artistic works. This complicates matters, and the proper interpretation of Kant has been the subject of extensive discussion and debate over a very long time. Here, however, it is sufficient to note that Kant has often been invoked as the author of the philosophically most sophisticated grounding for the ideal of artistic autonomy, an ideal neatly captured in the slogan "art for art's sake."

[17] Another subject to be returned to in Chapter 5.

Without entering into detailed examination of Kant's text, we may plausibly say that what I shall call the "Kantian aesthetic" holds that art is distinctive for having "purposefulness without purpose."[18] That is to say, when we contemplate a work of art we find within it order and pattern that give "sensuous presentation" to "aesthetic ideas."[19] In this way, a work of art may be contrasted with beautiful things that are simply the outcome of causal processes – glorious sunsets or stones beautifully polished by tumbling streams, for instance. It is in this sense that works of art have *purposefulness*. Yet, though they are indeed purposefully ordered and arranged, they may also be contrasted with machines. Like works of art, machines are intentionally created, but the ordering of their parts is not merely purposeful; it is intended to serve a specific *purpose*. A machine may be very ingenious, but if it does not serve the purpose for which it was made, or serves it very badly, it is a failure. A work of art, by contrast, cannot fail in this way. That is because, though it has *purposefulness*, it has no *purpose*. The significance of art is to be found in its form, not its function.[20]

In the light of this "Kantian aesthetic" it is easy to see that art properly so called must be distinguished from design. However elegant a designed object might be, it has purpose as well as purposefulness. The same way of thinking can be made to explain the difference between high art and folk art. Since works of art have purposefulness, but no purpose, the sole reason we could have for attending to them is their ability to sustain aesthetic experience. We delight in their elegance, charm, beauty, order, ingenuity, and so on for its own sake, and not for any further benefit we might obtain. To want or expect works of art to serve any other end or purpose is to fail to treat them as valuable in and for themselves. This is a failure that can take more or less gross forms. Everyone can agree that it would be a gross error to regard the royalties earned by a great novel or a great symphony as the principal source of its value. But if the Kantian aesthetic is right, though it may be less gross an error, valuing novels and symphonies primarily as sources of entertainment and recreation is equally mistaken. So that is what explains the difference between "high" art and "folk" art. The value of folk art *does* lie in the entertainment and recreation it affords to those who engage in it.

[18] Immanuel Kant, *Critique of the Power of Judgment*, trans. Paul Guyer and Eric Matthews (Cambridge: Cambridge University Press, 2000). First part §§ 10–11

[19] Kant, *Critique* §49

[20] "Significant form" is the concept specially associated with Clive Bell author of *Art* (1914), perhaps the most ardent exponent of what I am calling "the Kantian aesthetic."

What then is the place of art properly so called in human life? The answer the Kantian aesthetic gives is that once we lay aside all (allegedly) extraneous purposes, and attend to works of art entirely for the sake of doing so, art becomes a form of the *vita contemplativa* – the contemplative life. The expression *vita contemplativa* has religious roots. Its first appearance seems to have been in the title of a manual for monks composed in the fifth century. As this suggests, the contemplative life originated as a religious ideal, the sort of life that retreats from the world in order to devote itself to prayer and meditation on the divine. Some such ideal can be found in almost all the world's religions – the Buddhist monk, the Hindu sadhu, the Jewish mystic, the Muslim sufi, as well as Christian monks and nuns. This being so, it is not hard to see why the promotion of aesthetic contemplation might easily come to be regarded as an *alternative* to traditional religion, and so be expected to fill the vacuum that Nietzsche predicted the decline of religion would create. One important question, of course, is whether the word "contemplation" means the same in both contexts. Religious contemplation is usually taken to involve an attitude of complete *devotion*. In art, on the other hand, all that seems to be required is an attitude of close *attention*.[21] However, for present purposes the central question is not whether art is an adequate substitute for religion, but whether we have good reason to regard aesthetic contemplation as the uniquely fulfilling purpose of art.

Painting, Purpose, and Performance

One notable feature of the concept of "Art" that shaped the artworld was the pre-eminence of visual art, which was widely taken to be the paradigm for "high" art of every kind, and indeed a template for the other arts to follow. Thus, the earliest academies of "fine arts" were actually academies of painting and sculpture. As already observed, ballet was thought to raise dance above the level of the barnyard or the ball room by transforming it into "painting in movement." Similarly, musical composition was construed as "painting in sound." Drama, too, can be made to fit this mold if the actors are thought of as principally agents through whom the play – an art work emanating from the free play of the playwright's imagination – is given spatio-temporal existence.

This assumption – that *all* the arts bear some deep affinity to *visual* art* – has played a large part in promoting and sustaining, implicitly more

---

[21] For further discussion of this and related issues see Graham 2007, especially Chapter 3.

often than explicitly, the idea that the only valid attitude to art is one of aesthetic contemplation. It is indeed rather natural to think that our approach to beautiful paintings and statues should be contemplative; to appreciate them properly we need to stand still and give them our full attention. So if the other arts are rightly modelled on the visual arts, then it seems that appreciating them aesthetically will require us to contemplate them also.

Plausible though this contention may appear, there is one obviously problematic case, namely architecture. To a degree Kant himself acknowledged the difficulty of accommodating architecture within his "critique of judgment," though he only addresses it briefly.[22] The problem is that a work of architecture, it seems evident, *necessarily* has a purpose other than aesthetic contemplation. Buildings are functional constructions; they have a use. A building that had no purpose other than that of being aesthetically contemplated, would either be a beautiful ruin (the abbey ruins at Rievaulx in Yorkshire is a good example), a folly like those that were often constructed in the ornamental gardens (the "mosque' in Schwetzingen Palace garden, for instance), or a walk-through statue (Andy Scott's *Kelpies* by the Union Canal in Scotland is a case in point). These examples are all impressive structures, well worth visiting, but none of them is a work of architecture, precisely because they have "purposefulness without purpose." Yet if architecture properly so called is *both* purposeful (in the sense of having an intentional form) *and* serves some actual purpose, it cannot be classified as an art under the ideal of "Art for Art's sake"? It is logically possible, of course, to respond by denying that architecture is an art. This, though, seems to turn a philosophical theory into a dogma. It is impossible to ignore the fact that works of architecture, unlike more utilitarian structures, intentionally incorporate distinctively architectural features – columns, architraves, pinnacles, oriel windows, and so on. Architects use these features for the sake of their aesthetic properties – the charm, elegance, beauty, grandeur, etc. that they add to the building. If proponents of the Kantian aesthetic deny that architecture is an art, this means they have been driven to defend a theory in the face of all the evidence against it. On the other hand, if we do affirm that architecture is an art, it follows that *some* works of art are there to be *used*, and not merely *contemplated*. There is still the question, certainly, of how architecture's practical purpose is related to its artistic character (a subject to which we will return in Chapter 5) but asking this question

---

[22] Kant, *Critique* §14

already concedes that the art of the architect has at least these two dimensions.[23]

Architecture is not the only problematic instance. Treating the visual arts as a paradigm of all the arts makes this further supposition – that works of art are essentially *objects* of aesthetic contemplation. On reflection, this is a supposition that cannot properly accommodate the performing arts. The deep difference between painting and the performing arts is a major theme of a book by Friedrich Nietzsche that has already been mentioned, *The Birth of Tragedy*. A large part of Nietzsche's point in returning to Greek tragedy was to take issue with the Kantian aesthetic that was dominant by his time.

Unlike all those who seek to infer the arts from a single principle, the necessary spring of life for every work of art [Nietzsche writes], I shall fix my gaze on those two artistic deities of the Greeks, Apollo and Dionysius. For me they are vivid and concrete representations of *two* worlds of art, utterly different in their deepest essence and their highest aims.[24]

For Nietzsche, the Apollonian/Dionysian contrast is between the plastic arts and music, but we could extend it to include all the productive arts on one side – literature as well as painting and sculpture – and all the performing arts on the other – acting as well as dance and music. Nietzsche introduces the distinction in the course of dealing with several interrelated historical and philosophical issues, but only one of these directly concerns us here. What he wants to draw attention to is the fact that the Apollonian and Dionysian arts allow and invite different modes of engagement, the former passive and the latter active. The Apollonian arts produce images – literary as well as visual – which they invite us to contemplate. It is through looking, hearing, reading, and so on that we engage with them, and though there is more to be said about literature,[25] it is plausible to think that our engagement with them can be described as aesthetic *contemplation*. The Dionysian arts, on the other hand, invite performance in the form of dances, songs, plays, music. The basic form of engagement with these, is *participation*. Moreover, active participation is *fundamental* to these Dionysian arts. I cannot hear music that no one has

---

[23] Traditionally, architecture has been held to have three indispensable dimensions – "firmness, commodity and delight" i.e. successful construction, functional value, and aesthetically satisfying appearance.

[24] Friedrich Nietzsche, *The Birth of Tragedy*, trans. Shaun Whiteside, edited by Michael Tanner (London: Penguin Books, 1993) p. 76

[25] See Chapter 4

played, or watch a play which no one is acting. Aesthetic contemplation (if that is what the audience at a play or a concert does) is necessarily *secondary*.

When I look at a painting, or read a poem, what the artist has to offer me is in an important way complete. I cannot add to the painting or the poem without changing it. In the case of acting or playing music, however, what the playwright and the composer offer is incomplete. It *must* be added to. A script has to be acted, and a score has to be played. Without these actions, there would be nothing more than words or notes on a page. The relationship that human beings have with the Dionysian arts, consequently, is quite different to the relationship they have with the Apollonian arts. It follows that the Kantian aesthetic is mistaken on a second count. Aesthetic contemplation cannot be the one appropriate response to art, because there is more than one kind of art.

So far, then, we have seen that what I have called "the Kantian aesthetic" is seeking a unity in the arts where there is in fact important diversity. The contention that art has purposefulness without purpose and is pursued for the sake of aesthetic contemplation alone cannot accommodate architecture or the performing arts, and so cannot be sustained except by dogmatically excluding them from the realms of "Art." But even Nietzsche's twofold division does not adequately capture the diversity. Though literature can be put on the Apollonian side of the divide, it has its own differentiating features. Perhaps without too much distortion we could conceive of lyric poetry as "painting in words" – the production of images or "conceits" that the poet invites us to contemplate. But in epic poetry and in novels there is a different dimension – a narrative that we are invited to follow. Stories do include descriptions, of people and places, for instance, but these are rarely there for their own sake. Rather, they are one element in a larger narrative, and it is this narrative context that gives them their point. Of course, we might extract a literary description from its narrative context to savour its beauty and power. This does nothing, though, to show that the ultimate aim of the novel is "painting in words"; "narrative" is not a "pictorial" form, and can only be cast into this form at the cost of distortion. Furthermore, when writers use literary tropes – metaphor, metonymy, synecdoche, and irony, for instance – it is often to *mis*describe familiar things, in the hope that the reader will not simply savor them as they are, but come to understand something about them. In the case of a story, this process of understanding is extended over time. If we are to follow the story, it is not enough to contemplate what we are currently attending to. Occasionally, writers offer us what are called "stream of consciousness" passages. Even here, we cannot simply take in the whole with undivided attention, and have to remember what went before and connect it with what comes after. The need to do this is even more evident in a complex structure of plots and subplots. A story, in short, has to be understood in a way that a painting or sculpture does not. It is only a determination to stick with the Kantian aesthetic that could incline us to think otherwise, and falsely claim that understanding a story or a poem is only a preliminary to what ultimately matters – contemplating it aesthetically.

Art and Everyday Life

The "grand narrative of art in the modern world" that Wolterstorff identifies and rejects has both an historical and a philosophical component. The historical component is rooted in important social and cultural developments that took place in Europe between the seventeenth and the nineteenth centuries. These can be summarized as the emergence of a socially distinct artworld, with its own practices and institutions. The philosophical component is an accompanying theory, widely held, about the significance of this development. According to this theory, it is in the artworld that we find "art proper," which is to say, the fullest and most adequate expression of the essential spirit of humanity's artistic endeavors. The artworld's own autonomous institutions – museums, concert halls, academies, and so on – means that, now freed both from dependence on church and state patronage, and from the utilitarian demands of practical life, Art can devote itself to its proper end – the promotion of aesthetic experience for its own sake.

Since the historical development is an incontestable fact, it is the associated philosophical component that has been under scrutiny in the preceding sections. The conclusion to be drawn from the argument developed in them is this. Though the rise of a distinctive artworld really did bring something new and valuable into existence, what I have referred to as "the Kantian aesthetic" – the philosophical theory that has been constructed on the basis of that development (or alongside it) – is largely unwarranted. It is true that the presence of great national art museums, prestigious academies, and famous opera houses in the capital cities of the world has made "high" art so prominent and prestigious, we are very easily persuaded that it is the *only* manifestation of art. But this is not so. Art continues to be a presence in many areas of life beyond the artworld, and though there are terms available to mark off these other manifestations – "folk art" and "design," for instance – upon closer examination these do not reflect exclusive categories. Music is played, plays are performed, photographs taken, beautiful objects created, stories written, books published, buildings constructed, in many different contexts where aesthetic properties matter. Furthermore, even if it could be shown that the main, and possibly the sole aim of art museums, concert halls, and so on is to promote aesthetic contemplation for its own sake, this does not warrant the implication that art cannot have other legitimate aims. The existence of architecture should be a constant reminder on this point. It aims to create aesthetically pleasing buildings, certainly, but these are buildings for people to use, and not merely to look at or walk around. The aim of the composer and the playwright is to give people things to do, and not merely things to listen to. Bach wrote canatas for choirs to sing, and even an "art music" composer as great as Beethoven wrote piano pieces for the drawing room as well as symphonies for the concert hall. The great novels of Austen, Dickens, Stendhal, and Tolstoy were not self-consciously "art" novels, but even the authors of those that are, use their literary skill to inform and enlighten their readers, and not merely to provide them with examples of beautiful prose.

Perhaps architecture is most obviously an art of everyday life. It cannot be confined within some special viewing space, as a painting or a sculpture can. Rather, architecture shapes the spaces within which we conduct our lives – our homes, our workplaces, our public, and commercial buildings. Together, these buildings comprise town- and city-scapes, amidst many much more modest constructions. Something similar can be said about music. Though music can indeed be confined to the concert hall and to the iPod so that audiences and individuals give it their undivided attention, music is also a near constant presence in everyday life – street songs, ring tones, national anthems, buskers, parades, advertising jingles. Sometimes music is an irritating interruption, but it can also be an enriching enhancement to ordinary life. So too, while dramatic arts are most easily found in dedicated theaters and opera houses, the vast majority of people are far more likely to encounter drama on television and in the cinema. From time to time, too, people cease merely to be audiences, and become actors themselves, in high school plays, college reviews, and amateur dramatic societies. Visual art, of course, is everywhere – billboards, magazines, websites, statues, memorials, murals. A recent interesting development has been the movement to promote "public art," that is to say, commissions to artists to produce "high" art that is expressly intended for display in public spaces. Often the thought behind such commissions is aimed at bringing art out of the museum, and allowing those who never, or rarely, enter art museums to enjoy the kind of work they would find there if they did. A philosophically interesting question, though, is whether this change of location has itself an important impact on the nature and role of art. Can a representational statue or an abstract sculpture enter into ordinary life and remain essentially as it would be if it were in the museum? Works of art in public places do not easily allow the quiet sustained attention that they can be given in the art museum. In what, then, does their value lie as we hurry from place to place, eat lunch, or sit in congested traffic?

Once we cease to think of "high" art as the paradigm of art in general, we find artistic creativity and aesthetic interest in activities that are even more intimately connected with the conduct of ordinary life, the most obvious being the art of cookery. Human beings are unique in the fact that they prepare and cook their food. Unlike even the higher animals, they do not simply eat it as they find it. More strikingly, they have developed this practice in ways that reveal a concern with much more than appetite and nutrition. It is striking that the eighteenth century in looking for a word to encompass aesthetic discrimination in general used the word "taste," whose original home, of course, is in the world of food and drink. Philosophers debate about the extent to which cookery is to be regarded as an art,[26] but whatever we conclude on this score, there is no denying that when it comes to food and drink aesthetic properties matter to most people – color, arrangement, variety, texture, aroma can please as much as flavor and the ability to assuage hunger or thirst. Tending gardens, too, is another part of ordinary life in which aesthetic considerations can be taken to great heights.[27]

Philosophy, Art, and Religion

These observations allow us to return at last to art and religion. The "grand narrative" that we have found reason to question has also shaped thinking on this subject. If we suppose that the purpose of "art," as it is exemplified in the concert hall or the museum, is aesthetic contemplation, and that the aim of religion is also contemplation, albeit of a different kind, we may be led to wonder whether these two forms of

---

[26] See, for instance, Elizabeth Telfer, *Food For Thought* (London and New York: Routledge, 1996), especially Chapter 3

[27] See David Cooper, *A Philosophy of Gardens* (Oxford and New York: Oxford University Press, 2006)

contemplation are spiritually allied, or in competition with each other. That, very often, has been the framework within which artists and theologians have sought to deepen their relationship, in the belief that their contemplative practices are mutually supportive in some way. But once we see that aesthetic contemplation is only one possible role for art, and that wherever we look we find that everyday life is shaped by the arts and infused with aesthetic values, then we can begin to think of the relationship between art and religion quite differently. Religion, after all, is not the special province of monks and mystics, for whom the *vita contemplativa* has special attractions. Moreover, too great an emphasis on contemplation, characteristically an activity of the individual, can distort our understanding of worship, which more frequently takes the form of corporate ritual, i.e. cooperative and collective *action*. Religion is not confined to the soul's search for, and meditation upon, the divine. It is one of the dimensions along which societies and individuals, at all times and places and at every level of social and economic development, have striven to conduct their lives. It not simply a form of *experience*, but a way of *being*. Though easily cast as "other worldly" – a description the emphasis on mystical experience reinforces – religion in most of its forms is deeply practical, and closely connected with marking the "rites of passage" – birth, sexual maturity, parenthood, and death – through which the course of life from cradle to grave can be structured and understood.

With this social and practical perspective on religion in mind, we should expect to find that here – as in cookery, clothing, homemaking, leisure, and so on – the things that people and cultures do in the name of their religion are suffused with aesthetic interest and call forth intensive artistic endeavor. And so indeed we do find. Everywhere, the arts of music, literature, painting, drama, and architecture have been put to religious use. Conversely, everywhere, holy scripture, religious worship, liturgy, and ceremony have been shaped in part by aesthetic considerations. It is only if we are unduly influenced by the slogan "art for art's sake" that we will discount all these phenomena as somehow less than "art proper." By so discounting them, we fail to acknowledge that many religious artefacts and actions are wholly valid expressions of aesthetic interest and the impulse to make art.

The term "religious art" as it is used today has a very narrow connotation. It usually means a small subset of the visual arts in general, paintings with an identifiable religious subject, or sculptures in recognizably religious poses, for instance. Those who see that religion has long been associated with music and literature and architecture as well, often try to broaden the term so that "religious art" is understood to encompass arts other than painting. But though this desire is understandable, since there is indeed a much more extensive connection, simply enlarging the reference of "religious art" accomplishes very little. This is because, in a deeper sense, there is no such thing as "religious art." That is to say, there is no collection of objects or artefacts that can be grouped together in this way. It is not a specific set of objects that is central to the idea of "religious art," but rather, the role that the arts play in the religious aspect of human life. Taking this contention seriously necessitates relinquishing a certain sort of quest – the search for the essence of "art" and the essence of "religion" in the hope of comparing, contrasting and relating the two. Instead, understanding the relation between art and religion invites a more phenomenological and anthropological approach. It requires us to look at the ways in which different art forms can and cannot be employed in the service of religion, as well as the ways in which religion may transform an art by adapting it to specifically religious ends.

This move away from the abstract to the more specific is in keeping with developments in philosophical aesthetics. For a long time, philosophers focussed on the analysis and explication of a rather limited set of topics, notably the definition of art, the nature of aesthetic experience, and the objectivity of aesthetic judgment. Over the course of the twentieth century, however, philosophical aesthetics broadened into philosophy of the arts, and increasing attention was given to philosophical exploration of the distinctiveness of the different arts and the conceptual problems peculiar to them. Thus, allowing for a few nineteenth century forerunners, most notably Hegel, philosophy of music, philosophy of the visual arts (including film), philosophy of literature, and philosophy of architecture can all be said to be products of the second half of the twentieth century. Each of these branches of aesthetics has a special interest when it comes to thinking about art and religion because sacred music, the use of statues, paintings and icons, liturgical and devotional literature, and the construction of temples, churches, and mosques, are amongst the most prominent features of religious life. They are also closer to the lives of most religious people than creeds or theological doctrines. If philosophy can illuminate the strengths, peculiarities and limitations of these art forms, then there is good reason to think that it will have interesting things to say about both the historical and the potential relationship between the arts and religion.

The next four chapters will return in more detail to some of the issues outlined in this chapter. Each will be devoted to one of the major arts, in the following sequence – music, painting and sculpture, drama and poetry, and architecture. In each case, some of the principal philosophical issues relating to the art in question will be laid out in order to provide a context within which some interesting issues that pertain more closely to sacred music, painting and iconography, liturgy, and the architecture of religious buildings can then be explored. The hope in each case is to show how philosophy of the arts can be an especially good discipline through which to seek a better understanding of the nature, point and purpose of religion. A shorter final chapter will set out some more general conclusions about the arts and religious life.

2

Sacred Music

Music has a very long historical connection with religion, having played a part in the religious worship of virtually all of the world's religions. The origins of Indian classical music, used by both Hindus and Sikhs, can be traced back to the Vedas, Hindu scriptures that date from 1700–1100 BCE. Records show that music was used for worship in the Jewish Temple built by Solomon around 950 BCE. In China, music had received official recognition as an important element in ritual by 1000 BCE, and its influence spread to many other parts of Asia. Chanting is integral to the practice of worship and meditation in Tibetan Buddhism. Even in religious traditions where music is not expressly employed, and may even be officially prohibited, it can be present in a disguised form. For example, while music plays no part in orthodox Islamic worship, the "adhan" or call to prayer undoubtedly has a musical quality to it. Even more strikingly, the widespread and highly valued practice of reciting the Quran at religious ceremonies is sufficiently intoned that it can in fact be written down in musical notation.

In some cases, religious music is very simple – just the human voice chanting, a bell ringing, or the beat of a single percussion instrument. In others, it is very complex and ornate, as in a polyphonic setting of the Christian Mass or the classical Indian raga. As these examples, suggest, religious music can be both transmitted by tradition and purposefully composed by professional musicians. Most often, religious music takes the form of singing, words sung rather than said. For several centuries, despite its origins in the Jewish Temple, Christian worship permitted vocal music only and rejected the use of instruments. "In place of playing the tympani," the great theologian Gregory of Nazianzus declared, "let the

singing of hymns resound." This preference for the human voice continues to be the mark of some Christian denominations. In places where
this restriction came to an end and instruments were used to accompany
words, it was not long before instruments came to be used on their own,
with the supposition that they could make a wordless contribution of their
own to worship. Religious music without words eventually became such
a familiar practice that purely instrumental music in some of its forms is
now readily identified as distinctively "religious music" – the pealing of
bells and the sound of the pipe organ, for instance.

It is an interesting question as to why there is this long association
between religion and music. Is there some deep affinity between singing
and worship? If so, is the affinity psychological – the human impulse to
make music and the human impulse to worship being connected in some
way? Or perhaps, as ancient philosophers sometimes thought, the association reflects a deep metaphysical affinity of some kind between musical sounds and the nature of reality? These are important and intriguing
issues, and we will return to aspects of them. For present purposes, however, a more immediate question is this: how does music serve the purposes
of religion?

Obviously, to answer this question we have to say something about
what those purposes are. Two familiar if somewhat vague suggestions
come to mind. One is that music intensifies the spiritual experience of
the individual. The other is that something in music makes it especially
well suited to the practice of worship. These two suggestions are evidently
related to each other, but they have importantly different emphases. The
first focuses on the worshipper, and the second on that which is worshipped. For this reason, it is worth exploring them separately.

Music, Spirit, and Emotion

There is no doubt that in some religious traditions the principal role of
music is to intensify the experience of worship. This does not happen
by chance. Rather, the acknowledged power of musical sound, especially
in combination with movement, is employed quite deliberately for the
purpose of generating heightened emotional states. A notable feature of
Pentecostal Christian worship, for example, is rapturous singing, while
in Sufism, a mystical variety of Islam, the use of rhythmic percussion in
combination with swirling dance goes even further, and induces a trance-
like state in the worshipper. Something similar can be found in Hinduism
where, it is sometimes held, music can be a path to the ultimate goal of

the Hindu, namely "moksha," which is to say, spiritual liberation from the endless round of re-incarnated existence. In less exuberant traditions, emotion can still play an important role. Gregorian chant and Anglican anthems generate an attitude of quiet contemplation in which the mind or soul becomes "enchanted" by beautiful sound so that the worshipper may be transported to a higher or purer level of consciousness.

Music engenders emotional feelings in human beings. We may be uncertain about the psychological mechanism involved, but the phenomenon is something we can both witness and experience. Since these feelings are often powerful, it seems obvious to many people that the value of music lies in its emotional impact, from which it naturally follows that the value of religious music must lie in its emotional/spiritual effects. But the value of music in religious worship is a philosophical and theological question. It cannot be settled by any straightforward appeal to our own experience or that of others, because this question can always be raised. Are the emotional experiences produced by music *properly* described as spiritual or religious? We cannot simply assume that the answer is "yes," because music is also used to ends that make no claims to spiritual or religious significance. For example, many people find the musical experience of attending a rock concert emotionally thrilling. The anticipation of such experience is what takes them there, but they are content, generally, just to think of this as "fun" or entertainment. Concertgoers who quietly contemplate a recital of beautiful music may hesitate to call it "fun" or classify it simply as "entertainment." They may instead describe themselves as being "uplifted." Even so, they do not have to think of this in spiritual or quasi-religious terms. Aesthetic pleasure is enough. Both cases, it seems, provide evidence for the claim that music has the power to arouse human emotion no less solid and persuasive than any examples we might find in religious contexts. Where exactly, then, does the difference between emotional effect and spiritual value lie?

One thought is this. Even if we call the rock concert "fun" and the classical recital "aesthetic pleasure," neither of them has any purpose beyond the experience each of them generates. In both cases, members of the audience are there for whatever it is they get out of the music, and nothing more. By contrast, in religious cases, music, it seems, is intended to direct the player or listener to something or someone that goes *beyond* the straightforward experience of the music itself. Suppose, plausibly, that this contrast is correctly drawn. Even so, the hope and expectation of "something more" would not make the use of music in religion distinctive. In military music, for example, people often find "something more"

than just music. They are deeply stirred by it, especially when it has patriotic associations. It is precisely because music can have emotional impact
of this kind that it is frequently used for political purposes, both good
and bad. When music arouses people to patriotic fervor, it is directing the
emotion that it stimulates to an end other than simply a response to the
music itself. So it has a purpose external to the music, but this fact does
not make it religious music.

"What passion cannot Music raise and quell?" the poet John Dryden
(1631–1700) asks in his *Song to St Cecilia*, the patron saint of music. The
emotional power of music directed to many different ends is a platitude of
poets in fact – romantic love, pride, sorrow, joy, anxiety. If this is true, then
however much we might find ourselves inclined to capture our experience of music with religious or quasi-religious language – uplift, transport,
enchantment, and so on – the distinctive function of religious music cannot be satisfactorily identified with its emotional impact. In other words,
the special character of religious music does not lie in its power to arouse
emotion. Lots of kinds of music have the same power, and from this we
should conclude that they have to be distinguished one from another in
some other way. The example of military music suggests one such way.
Music can best be classified as "sacred music," "military music," "easy
listening," "classical music," and so on, in terms of the distinctive sentiments and purposes to which the emotional power of that kind of music
can be directed.

How are those sentiments and purposes to be characterized? Patriotic
songs like "America the beautiful," "Rule Britannia," and "La Marsel-
laise," as well as revolutionary anthems such as "the Red Flag" and "We
shall overcome," arouse national pride and political fervor. What makes
it *national* pride, and *political* fervor? It does not seem hard to answer
these questions. The music is just one part of a wider social context, a
context that includes such things as electoral campaigns, party rallies,
political marches, civic ceremonies, international sporting contests, pres-
idential inaugurations, and so on. In other words, the music succeeds in
having more than merely emotional impact by being played or sung in a
context that enables those who play and hear it to identify it as having
political significance. And of course, over time, an association grows up
between the two such that, even taken out of context, the music continues
to have political resonance.

It is easy to apply this line of thought to the case of religious music. The
emotional experience the music generates gains its religious significance
from the context in which it occurs – such religious occasions as worship

services, funerals, penitential processions, and the like. Here too, as in the political case, over time conventional association enables us to identify the music as "religious" even when it has been removed from any of those contexts. It is important to observe, though, that these associations can also fade. This has happened, in fact, with many compositions that were originally written and performed for religious purposes but are now regularly included in concert hall programs. What began as "sacred" music comes to be more frequently played and listened to by people who do not make those associations, and so hear it simply as "classical" music.

 In the light of this fact, we should conclude that the connection between religious worship and musical sounds is contingent. That is to say, music is "heard" as religious not because of the intrinsic nature of the sound, but because of associations that it has come to have, and may lose. We are sometimes led to think that the connection is closer than this because music that was once widely regarded as "religious" can, in a wholly secularized context, continue to have emotional impact and may even sustain quasi-religious description. It was noted earlier, for instance, that such music is often described as "uplifting." There is nevertheless this difference. When religious people describe music as "uplifting," they intend not just to indicate a powerful subjective experience by which their mood is lightened, but to make reference to something objective that explains and validates their experience. Their mood is not simply altered by the music. Rather, thanks in part to the music, they have been able to enter into the presence of God or the Divine. It is this that "uplifts" them rather than the music itself. While it is not unusual for music taken out of the church or temple to go on being described as "uplifting," isolated from that context, such a description can only refer to a subjective emotional experience. It no longer has any reference to what T. S. Eliot called an "objective correlative" of the emotion.

There is no reason to doubt that concert hall recitals of sacred music for secular audiences can be moving, and even in ways that are properly described as profound. The mistake is to infer from this that it must therefore continue to be religious music. Since the sounds and their effects remain the same, we have to seek the explanation of this important change elsewhere. This brings us to the second of the two suggestions set out above. Music can properly be called "military" only when it is performed in a military context and directed to military ends – even if the very same music can be listened to with pleasure in other contexts. So too, music

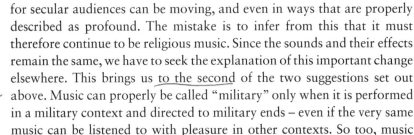

is properly religious when it is played in a religious context and directed to the worship of God, the Divine, or the Holy. Employing Eliot's term again, we may say that God is the "objective correlative" of the worshipper's subjective emotional experience. This raises an interesting question. If the emotional power of music is a means by which worshippers can access the Divine, it is easy to see why they should value it. But why does God or the divine grant access to worshippers *via* music? In order to access a locked room, I need to possess a key. Possessing a key is not enough in itself, however. The key must fit the lock. So we are compelled to ask: What is there about music that makes it peculiarly well fitted to worship?

The Nature of Worship

To address this question adequately, it is necessary to investigate not only the nature of music, but the nature of worship. With respect to this topic, though, we encounter an ancient philosophical problem. How is divinely directed worship even *possible*? This is an issue that is taken up, briefly, in Plato's short dialogue *Euthyphro*. Contemporary philosophical interest in this dialogue focuses mostly on the fact that it poses a dilemma about the relationship between religion and ethics. Is an action good because it pleases the gods, or does it please the gods because it is good? While this is the question that occupies the central section of the dialogue, toward the end, in what is possibly the least discussed part, a different question is raised, about the intelligibility of worship.

The Greek word *latrea*, which can be translated "worship," originally meant any service that might be offered or undertaken (usually for pay). This naturally covers the temple service offered by priests, and so by extension it came to mean worship of God in general. American English preserves this connection between worship and service, by referring to what goes on in church as a "worship service." So we might interpret Plato as raising this question – In what sense can worship be an act of service?

Euthyphro, the character from whom the dialogue gets its name, is reputedly a man with great expertise in the practice of religion. In keeping with many of Plato's dialogues, Socrates turns to him for help in discovering what true religious devotion, or piety, is. Euthyphro confidently answers his questions, but like many of Socrates's interlocutors, proves unable to resolve the philosophical questions and logical puzzles that their discussion uncovers. In the final part of the dialogue, Socrates wonders how human beings ever meaningfully serve the gods (or God[1]).

I am not quite clear [Socrates says to Euthyphro] about the thing which you call 'service.' I suppose you do not mean the sort of care we give to other things. The service of [God] is not like that – the sort of thing that we have in mind when we assert that it is not everybody who knows how to care for horses.[2]

Euthyphro, of course, can only agree. The service of God must indeed be radically different from anything as mundane as veterinary welfare. Yet, though he agrees that God cannot need *care* in any of its usual forms, Euthyphro has difficulty finding any basis on which to reject the general principle that "care is given for the good and the welfare of the object that is served." The problem, however, is that if we continue to subscribe to this general principle, and at the same time hold that worship is the service of God, we seem committed to the absurd consequence that God needs us to care for him. If true piety is the service of God, and if the point of service is to benefit its object, then the inescapable conclusion is that "when you do a holy thing you make some deity better."

This is an implication that Euthyphro emphatically rejects, yet despite his emphatic rejection, Socrates's point can hardly fail to impress the reader. It seems obvious, Euthyphro concedes, that the practice of worship includes such things as sacrifice and prayer. But if sacrifice is correctly described as "giving to the gods," and prayer is "asking them to give," then worship aims to be, as Socrates alleges, a "mutual art of commerce" between God and humanity. In this case, though, it is impossible to avoid the question that Socrates poses: "What advantage could come to God from the gifts which He receives from us? Everybody sees what *He* gives *us*, since every good thing that we possess is given by Him. But what advantage can He gain by what He gets from us? Have we so much the better of Him in this commerce that we get all the good things, and He gets nothing from us?" "Are you suggesting," a horrified Euthyphro asks, "that God *gains* anything by what he gets from us?" Yet if He does not, Socrates responds, we are at a loss to explain the meaning of the gifts we offer Him.[3]

---

[1] In the first part of the dialogue, Socrates shows that the gods have to be of one mind, so that the plural "gods" can unproblematically be replaced with the singular "God."

[2] Plato, 'Euthyphro' trans. Lane Cooper *Plato: The Collected Dialogues* edited by Edith Hamilton and Huntington Cairns (Princeton: Princeton University Press, 1989) p. 181

[3] Ibid., p. 184. I have substituted "God" for "the gods" and "He" for "them" here.

The problem Plato identifies here is a real one. What is it that is given to God when worshippers give him "thanks and praise" which, the ancient Christian *Sursum Corda* tells them, it is "a right, and a good and a joyful thing always and everywhere" to do? What does God get from human praises? Euthyphro is surely correct in rejecting the idea that God *gets* anything. Since God is the sum of all perfections, He can lack nothing. Consequently, He cannot lack anything that we might give Him. But if God gets nothing from our worship, what is the point of engaging in it? And wherein lies the obligation to do so? On the other hand, Socrates is surely also correct in his contention that we must have *commerce* with God. That is to say, a one-way transaction would not constitute anything properly called a relationship; if we are the *sole* beneficiaries (even on some heightened emotional or refined spiritual plane), we can no more enjoy a relationship with God than we can with the air we breathe.

Music, Worship, and Communication

As we saw at the start of this chapter, in most religious traditions music plays a large part in the practice of giving God (however God is conceived) thanks and praise. Consequently, to doubt the intelligibility of worship is to doubt the intelligibility of sacred music. The question, "what does God get from our music making?" is just a specific application of a more general question, the one that Plato's dialogue gives us reason to ask. Indeed, this specific version might be thought even more troublesome because it brings with it further problems of its own. The ancient practices of sacrifice are rather touching in their way. They show that often very poor people were willing to give God things that they themselves would value highly – the fatted calf, the new spring lamb, the first fruits of the harvest, the purest honey, wine or ghee, and so on. Still, however touching we may find this devoted generosity of spirit, such sacrifices are vulnerable to Socrates's challenge. From a human point of view, all these special, rare or precious goods are worth a great deal; from the divine point of view they are worthless. God has no need of food or drink, and consequently does not savor such things, even at their very finest. Once this truth dawns, such offerings seem relatively easy to abandon. Though there are parts of the world in which they continue, there is clear evidence that some ancient religions saw reason to abandon them. "Your countless sacrifices, what are they to me?" the Jewish prophet Isaiah declares on God's behalf. "I have no desire for the blood of bulls, of sheep and of he-goats when you come into my presence. Who has asked you for all this?" (*Isa.1:11*, Revised English Bible).

In comparison with these mundane sacrifices, offerings of praise through the medium of sacred music seem quite different, and able to take us into spiritual realms far removed from the blood of ritually slaughtered animals or the smell of purified butter. Yet, if God lacks nothing, he does not need the music of Gregorian chant or Lutheran chorale any more than he needs roasted meat or fine wine. It follows, or so it seems, that despite all their evident differences, music in worship is just as pointless as burnt offerings and oblations of food. Music may indeed intensify the emotions of worshippers, but it is not any more effective at facilitating Socrates's "mutual art of commerce" between God and humanity than animal sacrifice.

Is this negative implication unavoidable? Are we compelled to conclude that God gets nothing from sacred music, however beautiful or moving? Before accepting this conclusion, it is relevant to ask what it is that *anyone* gets, when presented with a musical performance or composition. If we are clear about the basis of human responses to musical offerings, this might enable us to say something about God's response. So what do concert audiences get from the music they listen to, and what does this say about its value to them?

For anyone putting together a concert program this is a practical and not merely a theoretical matter. On what basis should the pieces included in a concert program be selected? It seems obvious to say that the program should be based on what concertgoers like, and that what they like is what moves them. Having focussed on the effect that music can be expected to have on players and listeners, however, the previous section concluded that emotional stimulation cannot satisfactorily explain the role or the value of sacred music. By parity of reasoning we may also conclude that emotional stimulation will not answer the concert programmer's question either. To put together a successful concert program, we certainly need to know what kind of music people like and want to hear. This need not be restricted to music that they find emotionally stimulating. Still, to make musical preferences, whatever their basis, the sole criterion for inclusion, would be unwarrantedly conservative and lead to programs that scheduled familiar music over and over again. Concert programs generally have (in the broadest sense) an educational dimension, and rightly so. They aim to stimulate new musical interests and preferences in audiences by presenting them with *unfamiliar* music. Since an audience's reaction to music it has not yet heard can only be guessed at, and cannot be known in advance, the criterion by which the inclusion of new music in the program is to be judged cannot be an existing like or preference for it. The criterion rather must draw on the music itself. Are these new and unfamiliar pieces of music *worth* hearing?

This is an importantly normative question. We are asking whether these unknown pieces are good enough for concert performance. That is not a matter of predicting what people will like, even if we could do so with confidence. To call the music good is to say that people ought to like it. They may well not – initially at any rate. Early receptions by both audiences and critics of what are now recognized to be some of Beethoven's finest compositions demonstrate that even the greatest music can be disliked intensely on a first hearing, and famously, the audience that heard Stravinsky's *Rite of Spring* for the first time, hated it so much that they rioted! Conversely, music that delights its audiences may pall after a time. This, it seems, was true of the music of Mozart's contemporary Antonio Salieri. His many compositions appear to have so delighted the audiences who first heard them that Salieri was among the most heralded composers of his day. Yet they do not have much musical worth, so that within a few years of his death they disappeared from the concert repertoire, and there are almost no modern recordings of them in existence.

Audience reaction, then, whether positive or negative is strictly irrelevant to judgments of quality. Music is not good because we like it. Rather, we come to like it because we have listened to it attentively, not just once but many times, and judged it to be *worth* listening to. It only sustains and rewards the concentration that attentive listening many times requires, because it is *good* music. If it were trite or pedestrian, we would stop listening. So what the concert scheduler needs, accordingly, is not knowledge of audience reaction, but an understanding of what it is that an audience can expect to gain from music.

What then should we expect good music to give us? It has been widely supposed that there is an obvious answer to this question – communication. Music, we have already acknowledged, can stimulate moving emotional experiences. But its distinctive function, so it has often been suggested, is not merely to stimulate but to *communicate* such experiences. Communication adds something importantly different to simple causation. Making someone angry is not the same as "communicating anger" because the emotional content of what I communicate, and the emotional effect that it has, can be quite different. Suppose I am in a towering rage, and communicate my anger fluently and powerfully. The emotional effect on other people is more likely to be fear than anger.

Similarly, communicating my grief effectively is more likely to raise sympathy than sadness. The same point can be made about an earlier example. The power of a national anthem to arouse patriotic feeling depends on it being heard by those whose anthem it is. The music does not *communicate* emotion; it simply *triggers* it. And, as in this instance perhaps, music can have different emotional effects on different groups of people. The very same anthem that arouses pride in the hearts of some, might engender fear or hatred in the hearts of others.[4] We may conclude, consequently, that communicating emotion is conceptually distinct from causing it.

A great many people think that music communicates emotion by expressing it, or by being expressive of it. The subject is philosophically complex and not one to be investigated at length here.[5] That is because, for present purposes the general idea of music as a form of communication opens up other possibilities. There is no reason to think that music's communicative power is confined to communicating emotion. If music is indeed a distinctive medium of communication, perhaps it can communicate thoughts as well as feelings. Music's close association with emotion lies at the heart of a recognizable view in philosophical aesthetics sometimes known as "expressionism," and also strongly influenced the composition of music in the Romantic era. Indeed, the existence of music created under this influence does much to explain expressionism's widespread and continuing appeal to people who know little or nothing about the philosophy of music. It seems impossible to hear compositions by Schubert, Tchaikovsky, or Mahler without a sense that their music strives to *communicate* emotion. It is a small step from this to thinking that it is in this communication that the value and importance of the music lies.

Yet before the era of Romantic music, a different idea was found no less persuasive. The view sometimes known as "representationalism" holds that the medium of music can be used to communicate images, thoughts, and concepts by the sonic representation of sights and sounds – storms, waterfalls, shepherds, moonlight, battles, horses, and so on. All these examples fit easily into the associated conception of music as "painting in tones." But according to a more ambitious version of representationalism, music also has the power to communicate abstract ideas,

---

[4] Consider the case of the German national anthem. The original opening line 'Deutschland, Deutschland über alles' (Germany, Germany above all else) came to be so identified with Nazi excesses, that the current anthem omits the line completely and includes only the third verse.

[5] For further discussion, see Gordon Graham, *Philosophy of the Arts: An Introduction to Aesthetics* 3rd edition (London and New York: Routledge, 2005) Chapter 5

and even "*Weltanschauungen,*" global attitudes to human existence. It is this view, presumably, to which Beethoven meant to give assent when he declared that "Music is a higher revelation than all wisdom and philosophy."[6] Some writers have gone even further, and claimed that with respect to abstract ideas and concepts, music is actually a *more* powerful medium than words. It is a belief something like this that Felix Mendelssohn espoused, when he said in a letter to a friend that music can communicate "thoughts too definite for words."[7]

Expressionism and representationalism have different emphases – the first on feelings and emotions, the second on images and ideas – but they embody the same basic thought – that music is a communicative medium, which is to say a special kind of language. Viewed in this way, it seems easy to attribute a role to music in religious worship. It can serve both as a means of communicating the emotional attitudes of the worshipper – love, penitence, sorrow, joy, and so on – and as a means of affirming key theological beliefs. J. S. Bach's sacred music, it has often been claimed, is especially remarkable in both respects; the arias and chorales of his *Passions*, for instance, wonderfully capture and communicate love and sorrow, while the harmonic structures in his organ works can be interpreted as embodying theological doctrines.[8]

Plausible though these suggestions may be, the philosophical coherence of music as a communicative medium is a subject of considerable debate. Should it prove defective as a philosophy of music, obviously, it must be equally defective as a philosophy of *sacred* music. It is worth repeating that the move from "causing emotion" to "communicating emotion," is very important. The contention that it is of the essence of music to stimulate feeling, though widely accepted, is not as easy to show as might be supposed. Even if, for the sake of argument, we accept it, this does not give us reason to hold that music communicates emotion. The *communication* of the emotion does not require that it be *invoked*. Consider the case of ordinary verbal communication. I can grasp from the things people say, that they are grief stricken. I do not need to be

---

[6] As reported by Bettina von Arnim in a letter to Goethe, May 28, 1810

[7] *Letter to Marc-André Souchay,* October 15, 1842

[8] On this issue see the essays by Robin Leaver and John Butt in *The Cambridge Companion to Johann Sebastian Bach* ed. John Butt (Cambridge: Cambridge University Press, 1997); Calvin R. Stapert, *My Only Comfort: Death, Deliverance, and Discipline in the Music of Bach* (Grand Rapids: Wm B Eerdmans, 2000); and Karol Berger, *Bach's Cycle, Mozart's Arrow:* An Essay on the Origins of Musical Modernity (Berkeley, Los Angeles, and London: University of California Press, 2007)

stricken by grief myself. This is true even if we suppose (though there are reasons against such a supposition) that understanding how they are feeling must make us sympathetic. It is *understanding*, not *feeling*, that enables me to sympathize with them in their grief. So even if we do not doubt that music can generate emotion, we can still doubt whether it generates understanding. If it does, then that must be by means of what it *says*, not by means of what it makes us feel.

Now just what a piece of music as such "says" turns out to be highly elusive. Words, obviously, convey meaning. Consequently, to appreciate the elusiveness of musical "meanings" properly, we should concentrate our attention on purely instrumental music, and sever any connection with words. This is hard to do. It is no accident that in his once famous book *The Language of Music*, Deryck Cooke rests his case for music as a language entirely on examples of musical phrases accompanying words.[9] Without words, the "meanings" he attributes to musical phrases are much less obvious. Even if we set this difficulty aside, and suppose that some compositions can properly be said to have definitive semantic content – that is to say, that they unmistakeably represent specific scenes, objects, people, or ideas – this still falls short of their being truly communicative. That is because there is no obvious equivalent of the syntax by which their semantic content can be given different interpretations. The statement of musical equivalents to words and phrases is insufficient to display or to generate understanding. Understanding amounts to much more than naming or representation, and involves framing thoughts *about* the things named or affirmed, thoughts whose truth or cogency can be considered. For instance, in his book *Art in Action*, Nicholas Wolterstorff contends that "there is probably no better way to apprehend the character of angels than to listen with care to Messien's [*Les Anges*]."[10] Suppose this is true, there is still a crucial logical gap because the music has no way of telling us whether to affirm or to deny their existence or theological importance. However successful our "apprehension" of angels, the music cannot tell us what we ought to think about them.

Hanslick and Formalism

The arguments about music as a language cannot be settled in a few short paragraphs. Enough has been said, however, to show that there are good

---

[9] Deryck Cooke, *The Language of Music* (Oxford: Oxford University Press, 1959)
[10] Nicholas Wolterstorff, *Art in Action: Towards a Christian Aesthetic* (Grand Rapids: Wm B Eerdmans, 1980) p. 98

grounds for hesitating to endorse what has become quite a widespread view of music. Such hesitation gains further support from the fact that the first extended work in philosophy of music was a sustained attack on both expressionism and representationalism. This was Eduard Hanslick's nineteenth century classic *Vom Musikalisch-Schönen*, (*On the Musically Beautiful*), first published in 1854. "Whoever wants to learn about the objective nature of music," Hanslick writes on the opening page, "wants to get out from under the dubious authority of feeling." Hanslick thinks that expressionism and representationalism about music are commonly intertwined within this "dubious authority." Expressionism claims that the aim of music is to arouse feeling; representationalism claims that it is feeling that music chiefly represents. The difference, however, is not ultimately a significant one because both claims make the same mistake, or so Hanslick argues. Expressionism and representationalism equally locate the significance of music in *non-musical* content. They thereby inevitably fail to do justice to its being *music*. In affirming the general truth that "every art has as its goal the externalization of an idea actively emerging in the artist's imagination" they fail to see that "in the case of music, this idea is a *tonal* idea, not a *conceptual* idea translated into tones."[11] Nor, we can add, is it an emotional experience translated into tones. "The material out of which a composer creates…is the entire system of tones, with their latent possibilities for melodic, harmonic and rhythmic variety…The content of music is tonally moving forms."[12]

Hanslick's principal contention, then, is that the content of music *is music*. This sounds like an empty tautology. Who could deny it? Yet its tautological nature is its strength. Expressionism and representationalism in different ways deny it, but it cannot *meaningfully* be denied. Music is just music. The proponents of these philosophical theories cannot rest content with tonal ideas. That is why they go in search of musical value and significance beyond music itself. They seek the "meaning" of music in the biographical experiences of the composer, the emotional response of the audience, the non-musical images and ideas that the music represents or conveys, or some combination of these. Such theories are not simply philosophical inventions. They reflect and articulate a recurrent tendency that people have when they think about music. Yet, despite their popularity, against these theories and the inclination that prompts people to

---

[11] Eduard Hanslick, *On the Musically Beautiful*, trans. Geoffrey Payzant (Indianapolis: Hackett Publishing Company, 1986) pp. 31–2, emphasis added

[12] Ibid., pp. 28–9

espouse them, there is this altogether conclusive objection. If indeed it were the case that music is a "language," a medium of communication whose "meaning" lies in the non-musical content this language has the ability to communicate, then in principle, music could be replaced without loss by any other medium that can communicate the same meaning. If the value of Beethoven's *Pastoral Symphony* lies in its ability to conjure up images of shepherds and their pipes, a painting of the same scene would do as well. If it is said (following Mendelssohn) that music can convey "thoughts too definite for words," this makes no essential difference. A gesture or a look can convey a meaning that it is impossible to put into words. The meaning still transcends the gesture. The problem is this. Once we attribute content to music that is more than tonal, then what the music has to offer can be conveyed and apprehended by some *other* means of communication – verbal or visual. In that case, however, we can actually dispense with listening to music, and read its "message" in a book or see the images it "depicts" in a painting. It is Hanslick's important insight that this is a necessary implication of all versions of expressionism and representationalism, and he regards it as *reductio ad absurdum* of any theory of music that by implication renders musical sounds redundant. And so indeed it must be. Any theory of this kind effectively converts music from an autonomous art form into something like Morse Code – a system of sounds without intrinsic interest, that may, or may not, be more effective than other ways of sending a message.

In accepting Hanslick's contention, we need not deny that words can be used to convey a lot about a piece of music, and used, even, to capture some ideas and emotions that the music suggests. This is often what is happening in program notes and reviews of concerts. Words written *about* the music can be valuable because they enable people who have not (yet) heard it to listen more attentively when they do. A program note or a concert review might dissuade us from attending a recital, but it would not do this in virtue of being a substitute for listening to the music itself. *Nothing* can be a substitute for that. The burden of Hanslick's argument is that there are familiar ways of thinking about music that make such substitution possible in principle, and it is the absurdity of this implication that gives us good reason to reject all such ways of thinking. Wherever it is we suppose the meaning and value of music lies, the one truly distinguishing feature that we cannot relinquish is this: music has to be heard.

All philosophies of music rest upon the supposition that music is not just noise; it is *meaningful* sound. The concepts of emotional experience and revelatory wisdom are invoked by expressivism and representationism to explain music's meaningfulness, and hence its value and significance in human life. If Hanslick's rejection of all such appeals is warranted, how is the value, meaning, and profundity of musical sound to be explained? Now from one point of view, there is no explanation, or at least no explanation of the kind that people often seek. In so far as this is true, however, it is not troublesome. We can just take it as given, Hanslick thinks, that human beings find interest in the system of musical tones. This is unsurprising since the possibilities it has for melodic, harmonic, and rhythmic invention are astonishing. From another point of view, though, there *is* an explanation of its value. Music is unique in its ability to create beautiful sound. This is a form of beauty, and of creativity, that has no counterpart anywhere else.

Art should not slavishly imitate nature; it has to transform it …The painter is moved to artistic representation by the occasion of encountering a delightful landscape, a group of people …the poet by an historical event or personal experience. But what is there in nature that a composer could point to and exclaim: 'What a splendid prototype for an overture or a symphony!' The composer cannot transform anything; he must create everything new …which has no counterpart in nature and hence none in the other arts, indeed none in this world.[13]

Even the purest phenomenon of the natural auditory world, namely birdsong, stands in no relation to human music …[14]

I shall call the view that Hanslick is expounding here "formalism." The reason is that, on this account music properly so called has neither expressive nor representational content, but is a pure form. That is why Hanslick says it must "create everything new." Formalism of this kind is frequently rejected because it is thought to make music an arid intellectual exercise. Deryck Cooke voices this objection when he writes that "by regarding form as an end in itself, instead of a means of expression, we make evaluations of composers' achievements …largely irrelevant and meaningless."[15] But underlying Cooke's objection is the supposition that what is purely formal is necessarily *contentless* in the sense of "empty." This is false. The formalist contention is that music's form *is* its content. At first this sounds confusing or even contradictory, but it is

[13] Ibid., p. 74
[14] Ibid., p. 71. I think that Hanslick is right when he denies that the "song" of the birds is not music. There are some composers – perhaps most notably Olivier Messiaen – who think otherwise. But I shall not argue the point here.
[15] Cooke, *The Language of Music* p. 5

neither. The point is that though form and content are *distinguishable* in music, they cannot be *separated*. The mistake is to suppose that if two things are distinguishable, they must be separable. Convex and concave are distinguishable features of a geometrical curve, but they cannot be separated. A convex curve is distinct, but inseparable from a concave one.

Now just as the properties of a convex curve are different from the properties of a concave curve, so the properties of tonal content are different from the formal relationships between the tones. Furthermore, it is in no way improper to describe tonal content in non-formal terms. Describing the difference between two chords as "major" and "minor" uses formal terms. Describing them as "happy" and "sad" uses non-formal terms, and more adequately conveys something about the experience of hearing them. Nevertheless, though in this way we can *distinguish* between the sound of the chord and its structure, we cannot separate the minor chord and the sad chord. They are one and the same.

In order to specify the precise content of a piece of music we have to use formal terms – the melodic intervals, the chord sequence, rhythm, modulations of key, instrumental *timbre*, etc. – and it is by use of these terms that we analyze and identify musical forms. Such forms exist as music, however, only insofar as they are filled with tonal content. A Gm chord is a harmonic structure distinguishable from its tonal content. But the tonal content is nevertheless inseparable from the structure because, arranged in a different structure, the tonal content necessarily sounds different. Any change in the formal relationship between the tones must result in a different tonal content. Form and content, consequently, invariably go together.

Making and Performing Art

We may summarize the conclusion of the previous two sections in this way. The principal reason to favor formalism in the philosophy of music is that it gives proper weight to the uniqueness of music. This uniqueness is double sided. Since music is for listening to as nothing else is, hearing it is essential to understanding it. By the same token, since nothing can replace music, there is nothing beyond the music that it can be said to *stand for*. The language of emotion can certainly be used to describe pieces of music, but this fact should not be allowed to mislead us into thinking that music is a medium for the expression of emotion. Similarly, while music can properly be described as profound, we would be wrong to infer from this that its value lies in the revelation of deep thoughts. Music has no content other than itself.

Hanslick, as we saw, is fiercely critical of any conception of music that seeks to find non-musical content in it. Yet in a different way, he shares with those whom he criticizes another erroneous belief about music, namely that music can be characterized by the distinctive kind of arte-fact composers make. He shares the supposition that just as painters pro-duce pictures, and poets produce poems, so composers "produce" pieces of music.

The starting of all the creative activity of the composer is …the devising of a par-ticular melody. Through this deep-seated, mysterious power, into the working of which the human eye will never penetrate, there resounds in the mind of the com-poser a theme, a motif. We cannot trace this first seed back to its origins; we have to accept it simply as given.[16]

By writing in this vein, Hanslick is implicitly subscribing to a view that takes "art" music – the music of the composer and the concert hall – to be music's ideal type. In turn this implies that musical *works* are primary, and musical *performances* secondary. Such a view is an extension to the case of music of the "invention of Art" recounted and discussed in Chapter 1. In the case of music, we can note some important developments that led to "art music" having this special status.[17] Perhaps the most important of these was the development of musical notation. Music existed for a great many centuries before anyone invented an effective means of writing it down. In the absence of notation, music was simply *made*, and repeated only insofar as it was remembered. The invention of musical scores brought about a radical change. It opened up the possibility of singing and playing music that singers and instrumentalists had neither improvised for themselves nor heard someone else play. The invention of notation brought the very idea of "a composition" into existence. In time, this generated a further possibility – the composer as musical artist. With notation, different compositions could be known to come from a single and identifiable source. This, combined with the invention of print-ing, meant musical compositions from the pen of named "composers" became increasingly familiar, and grew to have a very important role in musical life. The rise of the concert hall intensified this. Concerts set space and time aside so that music could be an object of special attention. People were attracted to these occasions by impresarios who advertised "programs" of music in advance. The success, both commercial and

---

[16] Ibid., p. 32
[17] On this see Karol Berger, 'The Genealogy of Modern European Art Music', Chapter 3 of *A Theory of Art* (New York: Oxford University Press, 2000)

artistic, of the concert hall and the impresario then came to turn on "name recognition." Consequently, the fame of individual composers grew, to the point where first it equalled, and then it overshadowed the fame of performers.

It is easy to see how, at the end of this trajectory, "the composer" comes to be regarded as the principal artist in music, and the direct equivalent of the painter and the poet. Wolterstorff, in *Art in Action*, expresses (and endorses) just this view. "The fundamental fact about the artist," he says, "is that he or she is a worker in stone, in bronze, in clay, in paint, in acid and plates, in words, in sounds and instruments, in states of affairs. On some bit of the concrete materials of our stage he imposes order."[18]

This claim about a "fundamental fact" that unifies all the arts has been and still is widely endorsed. As we saw in Chapter 1, however, in *The Birth of Tragedy* Friedrich Nietzsche raises a dissenting voice. Nietzsche's distinction between "the Apolline plastic arts and Dionysiac music"[19] is intended to undermine precisely this assimilation of all the arts to a single foundation. If Nietzsche is right, the plastic arts and the performing arts are fundamentally *different*. The Apolline arts *make* things. The arts of painting, sculpture, and poetry create objects that embody visual, sculptural, or literary images that we are invited to contemplate with interest and delight. The performing arts of music and dance, by contrast, are Dionysiac arts. Their outcome is not objects that we are invited to contemplate, but *activity* in which we are invited to participate. The pulsating rhythms of dance music do not invite us to stop and listen; they invite us to take to the floor.

The validity of Nietzsche's distinction has been widely discussed.[20] In whatever way we interpret it, though, Apollo and Dionysus must not be understood to symbolize the different arts in a way that allocates them to mutually exclusive categories. Many people's experience of music, after all, is Apollonian. What they enjoy is hearing a tonal object expressly created by a named individual, as *something to be listened to*. When this is the case, the audience in the concert hall seems no less engaged in "contemplation" than the people who stand looking at paintings in the art museum. In both instances the object to which they give such close attention is a work originating from the imagination of an individual with a mastery of a particular medium.

---

[18] Wolterstorff, *Art in Action* p. 91   [19] Nietzsche, *The Birth of Tragedy*
[20] See, for instance, Julian Young, *Nietzsche's Philosophy of Art* (Cambridge: Cambridge University Press, 1992)

It is a mistake, though, to treat this Apollonian engagement with the music of the concert hall as the *paradigm* of musical engagement. Music is not simply written to be listened to; it is written to be played and sung. Indeed, though the invention and widespread use of recording tends to obscure this important fact, music *must* be played. A score is not music until players or singers literally *realize* it, that is to say, give it real existence as music. Without this realization, the listener would have nothing to contemplate. It is performance, not composition, that gives reality to music. The point can be made, not just about music, but about the performing arts in general. Consider the case of drama. Though people are often content simply to read Shakespeare, for instance, his characters require the realization that only the actor's appearance, voice, and gesture can give them. It is only in performance that a play becomes a reality, something that can be experienced.[21]

To this obvious, if not always evident, fact about the performing arts, we can add some further observations that are especially relevant to music in particular. While it may be true that most music – "pop" as well as "classical" – is written to be listened to, there is nevertheless a great deal of music that is *not* composed for this purpose. John Phillip Souza wrote music for marching to; Johann Strauss wrote music for dancing to; movie sound tracks are written, we might say, to be "watched to." More importantly for present purposes, most *sacred* music is not written to be listened to. Bach wrote a large majority of his works, not for recitals, but for *use* in church, a point that needs to be emphasized in a world that now mostly hears them at concerts.

It is also important to observe that a musical performance, uniquely, can lack both a composer and an audience, and nevertheless be a valuable enrichment of experience. Jazz musicians, for instance, when they improvise together follow no score and are not playing for anyone other than themselves, yet they are undoubtedly engaged in music making. The same is to be said of sacred music. Organists who improvise during the distribution of holy communion, say, are not following the musical inventions of a composer, but supplying a fitting aural context for a religious ritual by filling a sacred space with sound. Great musical skill is required for this. It is however, different from the skill of the composer. Composing a piece of music whose intrinsic beauty invites quiet contemplation in its own right would constitute failure, not success, in this context. It would draw the attention of communicants away from the reception of

---

[21] This topic will be returned to in Chapter 4.

the sacred elements, encouraging them to focus instead on the intrinsic beauty and interest of the organ music. The role of musical improvisation here is to enrich worship, not distract or detract from it.

Bearing both Hanslick and Nietzsche in mind, then, we arrive at a twofold conclusion. Following Hanslick, we may say that music is a formal, rather than an expressive or representational art. Its value lies in its tonal content, and not in what it makes us feel or think. Following Nietzsche, we may add that music is paradigmatically a performing art. That is to say, *making* music is primary, while composing music, and listening to it are both secondary. This puts us in a position to return to Plato's question. What does God get from human worship? A satisfactory answer can be formulated, I shall argue, if, following the arguments of the last few sections, we conceive of sacred music in terms of aesthetic formalism and ritual action.

Music and Worship

The opening stanza of a hymn by William Walsham How runs as follows.

> We give Thee but Thine own
> Whate'er the gift may be,
> All that we have is Thine alone,
> A trust, O Lord from Thee.

These are, no doubt, suitably humble sentiments to sing, but they do invite the question that Socrates presses in the *Euthyphro*. If, "all that we have" to offer is God's already, what is the point of offering it? Indeed, on what grounds can we intelligibly call it a gift? The conception of composers as producers of musical artefacts makes this issue especially difficult. Putting them on a par with painters, sculptors, and poets who make aesthetically valuable objects out of a variety of materials – stone, pigments, words – locates the value of what they do in the artefacts they produce from "tonal" materials. Human beings delight in artworks, but the "materials" out of which they are made, and the nature of those materials, flow from God's own creative activity. In that case, God *already* possesses the things we are trying to give, and this applies to tones as much as it does to matter of other kinds. On this way of thinking, the beauty of the artefacts we make is already present in the world that God has created, and artists "create" only in the sense that, by re-arranging the materials they use, they transform them in interesting ways. From such a point of view, however, it does not make sense to suppose that the inherent beauty of the materials is improved, still less exceeded, by the artist's re-arrangement. And indeed, some artists have expressly acceded to this limitation on their activity, claiming only to reveal what is there *already* in the materials on which they work. *The parts can make a better whole*

Confronted with this difficulty it is worth recalling Hanslick's contention about music – "The composer cannot *transform* anything; he must create everything new ...which has no counterpart in nature and hence none in the other arts, indeed none in this world." (emphasis added) If this is true, the objection we have just considered can be circumvented. Musical composition is a pure form of imaginative creation because musical composition is creation *ex nihilo*. This is contrary to what Hanslick's reference to the "materials" composers use appears to imply, but it resonates well with the unity of form and content by which, formalists claim, music is uniquely characterized. If form and content are inseparable, giving form to music is at one and the same time giving it content. The tonal "matter," in other words, cannot be separated from the musical "form" in which it is realized. In this respect, music is quite different from all those arts in which form and content are easily separated. When a bronze statue is melted down, for instance, the bronze "matter" out of which it is made is separated from the form that the sculptor gave it. The very same matter, consequently, is now available to be given another, quite different, form. What this shows is that, though musical composition is to be included among "the arts," it differs by nature from sculpture.

For present purposes, however, we can leave aside the issue of music's uniqueness, though it is a feature to be returned to briefly at the end of the chapter. For now, it is enough to conclude that music is a strictly formal art in the sense defined. It helpfully follows that music is not the re-ordering of pre-existent, divinely created matter. Consequently, a musical offering cannot be discounted as giving God back what was already God's. Rather, insofar as it is to be regarded in this light, it is offering to God something that human beings together (composer, player, singer) have called into existence.

This is just one important step in making sense of music in worship. More needs to be said, however, before we can conclude that Socrates's problem has been adequately addressed. Let us agree that the medium of music allows human beings to create *ex nihilo* and that, as a result, the offering of music in worship is more than the simple re-presentation of things that God has already given. Even with these claims no longer under dispute, there remains the question of why the presentation of humanly created music in the context of divine worship is to be regarded

as "service" to God. How could God need or benefit from *anything* that
human beings make – *ex nihilo* or otherwise? For all that has been said
about the uniqueness of music, this remains a salient question. Let us
summarize Socrates as asking, "What object could we give God that
he does not already have?" A formalist account of music avoids the
challenge of this rhetorical question because it gives us reason to think
that God does *not* already possess the music that human beings compose.
God has made the whole of creation, certainly, but necessarily, not those
things that human beings can create *ex nihilo*. Yet, even if this is the case,
how does God benefit from hearing the music they make?

This revised version of the Socratic question rests upon the "Apollonian" supposition that music is a productive art, and that musical
offerings are a variety of art *object*. As we saw, *pace* Nietzsche, this
supposition is not wholly erroneous. It fits the music of the concert
hall quite well. The intentional composition of musical works that are
realized by voices and instruments for the aesthetic contemplation of
audiences is a mark of the art music that has been an important part of the
artworld since the eighteenth century. The aesthetic contemplation of
music in the concert hall and elsewhere, is valuable because it enriches
the lives of those who hear it. Humanity is better off than it was because
the world now contains, as once it did not, the work of great composers
like Bach, Mozart, and Beethoven. A world that lacked such music would
be a poorer place. For all Nietzsche's strictures, this seems indisputable.
Yet, are we supposed to think that God could be enriched in this way,
that divine existence would be impoverished in the way that human
existence would be, if these composers had never created their musical
works? This seems a contention no less absurd than the supposition that
without animal sacrifices God would be lacking good food.

It follows that, while acknowledging the value and importance of
Apollonian art music, the Euthyphro problem will not be overcome until
we think of music more broadly in a properly Dionysian spirit. Now
setting aside for the moment any question about the value of music in
worship, there is good reason not to apply the Apollonian conception
to music in general. In many circles art music has come to be seen as the
pinnacle of musical accomplishment, but as was observed in Chapter 1,
it is in fact only one manifestation of musical life, and neither the most
widespread nor the most universally admired. Band music, dance music,
and folk music, as well as a great deal of sacred music, do not commend
themselves to people first and foremost as sources of aesthetic contemplation, but as spheres of activity in which they are invited to engage

by dancing, marching, playing, and singing. These are forms of *making* music, and not merely listening to it. Their existence thereby motivates a shift of focus from Apollonian musical *works* to Dionysian musical *performances*. In other words, we should think of music in terms of action rather than object.

How would this help? Surely, the Euthyphro problem simply comes round again in the original version – "How can our *actions* serve God?" It is true that the issue has not yet gone away. At the same time, by attending to music as action, some progress has been made. The distinctive nature of *liturgical* action in religious worship will be discussed at greater length in Chapter 4, but even in advance of that discussion we can note this important fact. Actions directed to others can be valuable, and valued, quite independently of any benefit or service that they render. Consider the simple action of saying thanks. It is appropriate to thank someone for benefits received, even if there is no thought or question of returning the benefit. Gift relationships, in contrast to exchange relationships, are necessarily one-way. That is to say, one party receives while the other does not. This does mean, however, as Plato appears to imply, that one-way relationships of this kind cannot constitute any sort of "commerce" between giver and recipient. On the contrary, human relationships are frequently sustained by gratitude far more than they are by exchange. Trade and contract are important, but they are not of any intrinsic significance when it comes to personal relationships. Business partners, lawyers and clients, politicians and civil servants may sometimes benefit from a personal relationship, but this is strictly unnecessary. It is enough that each side keep their part of the bargain.

Since the person I thank receives nothing except my thanks, the value of my action cannot lie in the consequential benefit he or she derives. Where then can it lie? The most plausible answer is that the value lies in its manner. I can undermine my gratitude by the way in which I give it. That is why it is possible to "empty" words of their meaning, even though what is said uses words from the dictionary and is grammatically correct. Similarly, words of welcome can be delivered in an unwelcoming way, and words of praise can be used to deflate and discount other people's achievements. These and a host of other possible actions show that sometimes the value of an action resides wholly in the *manner* with which it is performed. This important phenomenon is not confined to manners of speaking. The preparation of food is a distinctively human activity, and one of great value and significance. The way in which I serve food to guests matters greatly – carelessly, roughly, beautifully, messily, etc. – even when the nutritional benefit they can expect to receive from it is completely unaffected. Food poorly prepared and carelessly served may nourish the body just as adequately as the same ingredients elegantly presented.

These observations are of great relevance to the philosophy of sacred music. Let us agree that, while it may not be the only one, a key element in religious worship is giving God (or the gods) thanks and praise. Socrates rightly observes that God cannot benefit from this in any way, and wonders consequently whether divine service can have any point. What we have seen is that there are actions whose value does not lie in what they produce, but in the manner in which they are performed. So we can respond to Socrates with the observation that what matters is not *what* we give God, but *how* we give it. It is at this point that a special role opens up for music. The mistake is to think that sacred music offers God any *thing*. Rather, just as dance music, and military music shape and order human movement in ways that make that movement newly meaningful, so sacred music orders words and actions in ways that infuse them with a spirit of reverential devotion.

In the light of this, it is possible to see that the ancient impulse to offer food and drink to the gods is perhaps not as deeply mistaken as the stern words of the Jewish prophets and psalmists imply. The preparation of food is a uniquely human practice. It imbues the biological necessity of eating with a measure of grace and beauty and thereby transforms the act of foraging in a way that elevates human beings beyond all other animals. The German language marks this difference by using separate verbs for humans and animals eating. As far as our biology goes, we could survive and flourish by hunting and gathering. But since time immemorial we have not been content with doing so. In this sense, cookery may properly be said to be a spiritual art. It remains the case, of course, that cookery, even at its best, can only transform elements whose nutritional value must be taken as given. Music making is also uniquely human, and in a somewhat similar fashion transforms physical movement and the power of vocalizing. In the case of music, however, the formalism Hanslick articulates enables us to say a little more. Uniquely, music is a medium in which human beings can go beyond the transformation of pre-existing materials and create *ex nihilo*. In using it for the purposes of religious worship, therefore, human beings transcend their dependence upon the created world and enter more fully in the life of spiritual creation.

Conclusion

The ancient *Book of Psalms* has been used over many centuries by both Jews and Christians of every variety. It contains poetic hymns of praise that date from many different periods, includes several that urge worshippers to sing, and closes with a psalm that extols the use of instruments. "Praise God in his holy temple…Praise him with lyre and harp, timbrel and dance, strings and pipes, resounding cymbals." This is powerful evidence of a very deep-seated impulse, and long-standing practice, that turns to music as a natural vehicle of religious devotion. No one moved by this impulse has needed to wait for a rational justification or a philosophical explanation of its incorporation into religious liturgies. This fact shows that the arguments of this chapter are reflective, rather than prescriptive. The conclusions we have arrived at will not tell anyone how to compose sacred music or what music to include in worship services. Still, this does not make the philosophy of sacred music completely irrelevant from a practical point of view. There are better and less good ways of thinking about music, and its role in religious worship. Getting clear about the issues discussed in this chapter can enable worshippers to have a better sense of what they are doing and why they do it. It may even throw some light and offer some guidance on the kind of sacred music that is fitting in different circumstances and on different occasions.[22] The main purpose, however, has been to arrive at a deeper understanding of one enduringly important aspect of the relationship between religious faith and artistic creativity. In the next chapter, we turn to another aspect of the same relationship – religious faith and visual art.

---

[22] For a discussion of some of these more "practical issues" see Gordon Graham, 'The Worship of God and the Quest of the Spirit: 'Contemporary' versus 'Traditional' Church Music' in *How Shall we Sing the Lord's Song? – The Meaning of Music and the Song of God*, edited by Ben Quash, Vernon White, and Jamie Hawkey (London: Ashgate, in press)

3

Art, Icon, and Idolatry

Many religions are notable for the wealth of visual art they have generated. Indeed, according to the *Oxford Dictionary of World Religions*, it is
religions that have been "the source and inspiration of almost all the most
enduring art and architecture throughout the whole of human history, at
least until very recently."[1] As the inclusion of architecture in this claim
suggests, the assessment relates to the arts in general, all of which have
benefitted enormously from religious patronage on a massive scale over
a very long period of time. When people speak of "religious art," though,
they are often referring primarily to the visual and plastic arts – painting,
sculpture, ornamentation, tapestry, calligraphy, and so on. Even if we confine ourselves to these visual arts (the subject of this chapter), the *Oxford
Dictionary*'s claim still holds good. Leonardo's *Last Supper*, Michelangelo's Sistine Chapel ceiling, Bernini's statue of *St. Theresa's Ecstasy*, and
Rubens's *Miraculous Draught of Fishes* all have Christian subjects and
are at the same time famous, and sumptuous, examples of European
visual art at its finest.[2] Furthermore, it is also true that these works, along
with a great many others, owe their very existence to Christian patronage.

Christianity is not the only world religion to have produced great
art. Hinduism too has generated a huge profusion of vibrant painting,
ornamentation, and statuary. On the other hand, in sharp contrast to
these two world religions, Judaism and Islam are notable for their deep
reservations about visual art, especially of a representative kind. In

---

[1] John Bowker, ed., *The Oxford Dictionary of World Religions* (Oxford and New York:
Oxford University Press, 1997) p. 91
[2] All the pictures referred to in this chapter can be found on Wikiart.

Judaism, this reservation springs from a fear of idolatry. The second of the Ten Commandments given to Moses on Mount Sinai says, "You must not make a carved image for yourself, nor the likeness in the heavens above, or on the earth below, or in the waters under the earth. You must not bow down to them in worship." (*Exodus* 20:4) Islam shares this reservation, though for slightly different reasons perhaps. The *hadith*, which records all properly authenticated stories about the life of the Prophet Muhammad, recounts an episode in which Muhammad returned home to find that his favorite wife, A'isha, had been embroidering a cloth with human figures. He threw both the embroidered cloth and A'isha out of the tent, with the words "Give life to that which you have created." We may take this remark to mean that representative art is a sacrilegious (and of course fruitless) attempt to imitate the work of the Creator. No one can give life except God, yet representative art, on this view, falsely and foolishly suggests otherwise.

A tension between those who favor visual art and those who are suspicious of it can be found within one and the same religion. The Protestant Reformation gave rise to Christian denominations that rejected representative visual art for the same reasons as Judaism, namely its conflict with the Ten Commandments. Even Eastern Orthodoxy, a variety of Christianity generally marked by the brilliant visual beauty of its interiors, vestments, and especially icons, has a history in which the practice of iconography generated heated theological debate between "iconoclasts" and "iconodules" in the eighth and ninth centuries. Like the Jews before them and the Protestant reformers after them, the iconoclasts feared that the visual arts led Christian worshippers into idolatry and at a council held in 754 denounced "the evil art of painters." In the "First Iconoclasm" (roughly, 730–787), and again in the "Second Iconoclasm" (814–842), a great number of the religious images that filled so many churches were destroyed. The iconodules (or iconophiles), whose most articulate advocates were St. John of Damascus (676–749) and St. Theodore of Stoudios (759–826), regarded those very same images as both a valuable focus for Christian devotion and a source of spiritual sustenance.

One view of the relationship between religion and the visual arts, then, sees a deep affinity between the two, while the other sees an equally deep incompatibility. It is part of the aim of this chapter to show how such a difference of opinion arises, and to throw some light on a recurring debate about the use of images in religion. In order to do this, the next section will consider some of the philosophical and theological ideas that underlie these debates. Subsequent sections will focus on Christianity, and explore in more detail the contrast that is to be found between the visual art of the Latin West, and the iconography of the Orthodox East.

Appearance, Representation, and Resemblance

When we first begin to philosophize about the nature of visual art it is natural to think in terms of representation and resemblance. Painters and sculptors, we assume, are people whose skill in the use of pigments, stone, or metal enables them to represent objects, people, and places in pictures and sculptures that resemble those objects. Whereas stories and poems depict the world around us by means of linguistic description, visual art depicts by means of lifelike appearance. Now although this conception of visual art is so widely assumed to be true that it sounds like a commonplace, it does not take much reflection to see that, however obvious it may seem initially, it cannot be quite right.

To begin with, though figurative art is rightly thought to aim at the representation of things, it does not need to do so by means of resemblance, and in fact, often does not do so. In a lot of figurative art, representation is stylized. For instance, a very simple drawing can successfully represent a smiling or a frowning face, even though the few lines and shapes it uses to do this – convex and concave lines within a circle – do not add up to anything that much resembles a real human being. Similarly, cartoon animals, vehicles, and buildings successfully represent without any close resemblance to the real thing – no one would mistake Mickey Mouse for an actual mouse. It is an important and striking fact that even very small children can recognize the objects depicted in cartoons, despite the absence of anything that could plausibly be called visual resemblance.

Second, while it is true that some visual depiction strives to attain as close a resemblance as possible to the thing depicted, the purpose behind this striving need not be artistic, and generally is not. The assembly of an "identikit" picture based on the observations of witnesses is one obvious example. A lot of work goes into trying to get as close to the original in appearance as possible. It is true, of course, that identikit pictures are not "freehand" drawings, but use stock sets of facial features. Yet, this is not the principal reason for denying them the title "art." Even when real skill at drawing and coloration is needed, and the result is a beautiful picture, the primary aim may not be artistic. The illustrations found in guidebooks to birds and plants are often so well done that they are beautiful in their own right. Nevertheless, like identikit pictures, they have a practical purpose – enabling us to identify the species to which real birds belong. Just as drawings that do not look much like the criminal for whom the police are searching are deficient, so guidebooks that don't actually help us identify the birds or plants they depict are rightly discarded, regardless of how attractive or beautiful they may be.

Third, the most striking instantiation of representations that closely resemble by means of appearance is *trompe l'oeil*. This expression refers to a two-dimensional depiction that is so close in appearance to the original that it deceives us into thinking a three-dimensional object depicted is actually present. It is undeniable that *tompe l'oeil* requires an exceptional mastery of perspective, foreshortening, and the use of color, light, and shade. Such mastery enables the painter to create an intriguing and often convincing illusion. The result, however, is rarely an artistic masterpiece. On the contrary, *tompes l'oeil* are more usually considered curiosities. True masterpieces also show exceptional mastery of perspective, color, and so on, but to a different end. Vincent van Gogh's "Irises," for example, is a figurative painting that wonderfully displays his remarkable gift for shape, composition, and color. But no one would ever mistake it for a photograph, still less be deceived into thinking that there were flowers in the room where it was hanging.

The existence of *non-figurative* art such as abstract painting and geometrical design provides a fourth important counter to the idea that "representation by means of resemblance" is central to visual art. Abstract visual art does not strive for resemblance at all, yet it can nevertheless be representational, and in fact, some of the clearest cases of abstract representation are to be found in religious art. The *mandalas* that are characteristic of the religions of India, for example, are *both* abstract geometrical designs *and* symbolic representations of the cosmos. The Madhubani wall paintings of Hindu religion on the India–Nepal border are especially striking for their colorful geometrical patterns, though they also incorporate depictions of animals, people, and plants. These figurative elements, however, do not succeed in representing by virtue of their resemblance to the things represented because they do not look anything like the humans or animals we might see in the world around us. A similar point can be made about representations of the Christian Cross. No one really knows just what the cross on which Jesus was crucified looked like. Yet ignorance on this point is no obstacle to its being visually represented. On the contrary, the Cross has been successfully represented by a wide range of contrasting visual images – the Jerusalem cross, the Celtic cross, the Orthodox cross, and so on. All of them are recognizably crosses, but we are not in a position to say that any of them recreates the appearance of the original.

A fifth important consideration is this. Visual art that has no connection with either resemblance or representation may still have an important role in the decoration and ornamentation of churches, temples,
synagogues, and mosques – especially the last two, since the art that
Judaism and Islam make use of must not be figurative. Despite, or perhaps because of this restriction, Islamic art especially has taken geometrical design to extraordinary heights. Repeated and overlapping squares,
circles, stars, and polygons, are developed into immensely complex patterns in tiling, plasterwork, and carving. Potentially such patterns extend
indefinitely, and so can be thought of as pointers to infinity, but they neither resemble nor represent anything. It would be difficult to deny, nevertheless, that Islamic decoration of this kind is to be counted among visual
art's most astonishing accomplishments.

The conclusion to be drawn from these considerations is this. Though
initially it may seem obvious that the meaning and value of visual art lies
in its ability to resemble and represent, we should resist any impulse to
think in this way. Certainly, the art of representation by means of resemblance is an important artistic accomplishment acquired over many centuries, and nothing in the argument so far should be taken to diminish
or detract from that accomplishment. Still, the extent to which the representation of a thing needs to resemble that thing, is neither a criterion,
nor a measure of artistic excellence. Rather, it is a function of the purpose
to which the representation is being put. It is true that lifelike pictures
and photographs of things, people, and places are useful, especially for
the purposes of identification and record, and that is why human beings
paint pictures, take photographs, shoot film, and make models to record
and recall their experience. The point to be emphasized in this context,
however, is that representative pictures can serve many other purposes
besides these. Consider the case of film as a visual art, which is especially
notable in this connection. While film's first use was indeed to record
events, it quickly came to be much more than newsreel and widely used
for entertainment, education, commercial advertising, political campaigning, moral inspiration, and self-expression. Occasionally, the rationale for
film making was nothing other than visual enrichment in and for itself.
This multi-purpose nature may be less obvious with respect to the other
visual arts, but is not any less a fact.

It is a fact with some very important implications. Once we acknowledge that visual art can serve a wide range of purposes, it is easy to see that
many of these purposes may be served just as well by non-representational
art. The mastery of shape, color, perspective, composition, and so on, can

be used to give special impact to purely *abstract* art, in, for example, symbols, company logos, and complex geometrical patterns of the kind found in mosques and synagogues. In short, neither resemblance nor representation exhausts the possibilities of visual art, so that neither can be said to be its defining end or purpose. Rather, resemblance and representation are among the *means* that visual artists have at their disposal in pursuit of their work.

Once we grasp this point, our thinking about visual art must undergo a change. Having relinquished the assumption that the essence of painting, sculpture, and so on lies in visual resemblance and representation, we are free to ask what the ends are to which visual art's distinctive means can most powerfully be directed. One of these ends may be, as aestheticians have tended to insist, the creation of the visually beautiful for its own sake. But clearly, the other purposes listed earlier – entertainment, commercial advertising, education, political campaigning – can also be served, and enhanced, by visual art. We can now add religious purposes to this list, and this gives us a helpful conceptual framework within which to explore the relationship between the visual arts and religion. What religious purposes is it that visual art, given its nature, serves most effectively?

Visual Art and Religious Life

How are the aims or purposes of the religious life best characterized? This is both a difficult and a highly debatable question, difficult because of the dangers of overgeneralizing, and debatable because the answers we give to it cannot be separated from issues over which religious believers have frequently disagreed, sometimes passionately. In view of both the difficulty and the disagreements, any attempt to identify the core aims of religious life must be tentative and at best provisional, but it can still prove useful in organizing and clarifying the topics of this chapter.

Just as it is commonly supposed that resemblance is essential to visual art, so there is a common supposition that *belief* lies at the heart of religion. That is to say, it is widely assumed that religion is to be defined in terms of a belief in the supernatural. Religion, this assumption implies, is humanity's response to a reality that lies beyond or behind the world we ordinarily perceive. This is the same world as the one natural science investigates systematically, but because the spiritual world is *super*-natural, its transcendent reality is not something we can discover for ourselves. It has to be specially *revealed* to us.

As we will see, the centrality of *belief* to religion, is open to question, but it is not without reason. It receives significant confirmation from the fact that Judaism, Christianity, and Islam all regard their sacred writings – the Hebrew Scriptures, the Christian Bible, and the Quran – as the special "revelation" of a divine reality. That is why these three great monotheistic traditions are often called "the religions of the Book." The religions of the East – Hinduism, Buddhism, and Sikhism – also have their holy writings – the Upanishads, Buddhavacana, and Adi Granth – though not all of these are books of revelation in the quite same sense as the Quran or the Bible. Nonetheless, they too are crucial in shaping these religious understandings of the world.

Taken together, the adherents of the six great religions just listed comprise the vast majority of the world's religious believers. Still, not *all* religions have holy books, and even in the case of those that do, the religion in question can very rarely be said to be *founded* on its holy book. While there are occasional exceptions to this general rule – arguably, the religion of the Latter Day Saints was founded on the *Book of Mormon* – in most cases holy books *emerge*. The Christian Gospels, for example, were composed decades after the events they recount, and only became "canonical" some centuries later. Similarly, though the Quran consists in God's revelations to Muhammad, these accumulated gradually over a twenty-two year period, and were not collated and given unalterable authority until after Muhammad's death. By that time, the Caliph Uthman, who is usually credited with this accomplishment, was already regarded as a leader of Muslims. The historical origins of the Hebrew Bible are somewhat obscure, but most scholars agree that the books of law – *Exodus* and *Leviticus* – were composed *ex post facto* as the Israelites sought to re-affirm their ancient faith after the Persian conquest and their exile in Babylon. In all three cases, religious identity *preceded* the compilation of writings that were subsequently given the status of divine revelation. The Adi Granth – the Sikh holy book – is a compilation of the teachings and writings of the ten Sikh gurus. It only assumed the status of holy writ and became known as the Guru Granth Sahib at the end of an historical period, when it took the place of the tenth guru.

Since the significance of all these holy books is derived from the role they have come to play within a distinctive cultic practice, some students of religion have seen this as a reason to place the primary emphasis on religious *cult* rather than religious *belief*. The point is that, taken out of this context, "holy scriptures" become simply ancient texts, and while this may make them no less interesting to study, it deprives them of their authority as "revelation." It is only within the context of a religion that they can claim the status of scripture. That is because the propositions about the supernatural reality they reveal rely on a vocabulary and a set of concepts whose meaning has arisen within this practice. With both these thoughts in mind, it seems that religious *practice* must be regarded as more foundational than religious *belief*. Accordingly, or so it appears, we should conclude that the heart of a religion is to be found in its rituals, ceremonies, and ethical principles rather than its creeds and catechisms.

A third body of opinion is dissatisfied with both belief and practice as key to religion. This dissatisfaction has often rested on an awareness of the difference between religious faith and social custom or convention. From this point of view, it is a mistake to place all the emphasis on religious belief because subscription to creeds and doctrines may amount to nothing more than an intellectual assent to abstract propositions. On the other hand, participation in religious practice can be purely conventional, and its ceremonies *mere* rituals. When either of these things is true, somehow the religion in question lacks life, and just as expressions of feeling can be hollow, and physical gestures can be empty, so creeds can be recited and liturgical rituals performed without any of the spirit that transforms them into real religion. In view of the possibility, and danger, of "dead" religion, there does seem good reason to hold that the key to real religion must lie elsewhere. This thought has led many thinkers to lay the principal emphasis on religious *feeling*. What matters is the *spirit* of religion, an emotionally powerful experience of the supernatural or the divine, rather than either subscription to a set of metaphysical teachings or participation in ceremonial practices that have come to be associated with the religion in question.[3]

In recent times, this emphasis on the emotional basis of religion has received added support from the "cognitive science of religion" (CSR). CSR, which has an important forerunner in David Hume and the philosophy of the Scottish Enlightenment, explores the psychological basis of religion by means of empirical observation. When we systematically investigate the factors that generate and sustain a religious mentality, CSR tells us, we find that the real drivers are not the theological doctrines to which adherents may well say they subscribe, but rather a set of embedded psychological and emotional dispositions that incline human beings to understand and interpret their experience in religious terms. We are

---

[3] William James takes precisely this view of the matter in his famous Gifford Lectures, *The Varieties of Religious Experience*, first published in 1902.

misled on this point, according to some psychologists, by a phenomenon that has been given the name of "theological correctness." It has often been observed that a theological doctrine can be widely held to be essential to a religion and yet have little to do with the thoughts and practices of its adherents. The Christian doctrine of The Trinity is sometimes cited as a notable example of this phenomenon. All major branches of the Christian Church hold that subscription to the doctrine of the Holy Trinity is definitive of Christian orthodoxy. Yet the vast majority of practicing Christians would have great difficulty in explaining it, and still greater difficulty in identifying the difference that it actually makes to their conduct. What this suggests is that while "official" theological doctrines provide important badges of identity for the adherents of a particular religion, and thus serve to demarcate between religions, the *actual* source of religious motivation lies elsewhere and at a deeper psychological level.

These contrasting emphases – on theological belief, religious ritual, and spiritual or psychological motivation – have sometimes been construed as rivals, especially within the same religion. Islam, for example, has standardly made *practices* central to the life of a Muslim – daily prayers, alms-giving, fasting, pilgrimage to Mecca, and the observance of *sharia* (or Islamic law). However, from time to time theological questions and debates relating to the importance of Iman (faith) in the Five Pillars of Islam have gained considerable prominence, and over many centuries Sufism, whose interest lies in awakening mystical experience, has proved attractive to some Muslims, while drawing hostile persecution from others. Something similar can be found in Christianity. The thick accretion of ritualistic and liturgical practices characteristic of the medieval Church was swept aside by the sixteenth century Protestant Reformers in favor of written "Confessions" that specified the doctrines to which true believers must subscribe. At a later period, first the American "Great Awakenings" and then the worldwide Pentecostal movement reacted against both ceremony and theology, seeking instead to stimulate emotionally powerful conversion experiences that alone can bring meaning to both dead doctrine and empty ritual.

This threefold classification, traditionally referred to (in a different order) as "intellect, emotion and will," has prompted theological debate and religious division. Yet it is correct to say that it marks different *emphases* rather than separate categories. All religions have their distinctive practices, virtually all have teachings about the supernatural, articulated with widely varying degrees of sophistication of course, and every religion makes some appeal to the necessity for validation or confirmation in feeling and experience. Consequently, to classify the aims and ends of religious life in this threefold way is not to offer a phenomenal typology of religions. Nevertheless, it does provide us with a useful means in which to think about the different ways visual art serves religious ends.

Initially, this might not appear to be so. At first glance *none* of these contrasting emphases seems well suited to visual art. If we place the emphasis on belief and doctrine, it is literary art that appears to be the most promising medium for religion to employ – in its catechisms, devotional poems, sacred narratives, hymns of worship, and so on. If we place the emphasis on rituals, music, and drama seem to have the major role, especially in combination with the art of architecture that can be used to create and define the sacred spaces within which ritual is conducted. If the emphasis is given to personal spiritual or emotional experience, then music, dance, and poetry are the obvious contenders for artistic expressions of religion. It seems hard, consequently, to determine any distinctive role that paintings or statues could play in religious life, or even any role at all. In reality, however, provided we look more carefully, we can find visual art aligned with all three facets of religion. Visual narrative serves religious belief, visual identity serves ritualistic practice, and visual expression serves the life of the spirit. The next three sections explore each of these topics in turn.

Visual Narrative

There is a widespread inclination to think of religious beliefs as theological doctrines or ethical principles. Frequently, however, the most obvious and accessible religious beliefs take the form of stories – stories of divine visitations, miraculous happenings, conversion experiences, historical events. The Jewish religion is best summarized, in fact, as the story of God's dealings with the Israelites, of which the call to Abraham, liberation from enslavement in Egypt, the journey through the Wilderness to the Promised Land, the Exile to Babylon, and return to Jerusalem are key elements. For Christians, these same stories are crucial, but the narrative culminates in the story of Jesus – his birth, ministry, miracles, parables, passion, Crucifixion, and Resurrection. The Quran is unusual as a holy book that has no stories, but for Muslims also the figures of Abraham and Jesus have special importance, and of course episodes in the life of Muhammad have great interest and significance. Suitably authenticated, these are recorded in the *hadith*, which has a quite different status to the Quran, but to which immense importance is still attributed. Stories are no less important when we turn our attention to the religions of the East. The enlightenment of the Buddha as he sat under the Bo tree is the pivotal event of Buddhism, while the Hindu scriptures recount at great length the doings of Hindu gods and goddesses.

Scriptural stories involve important individuals. For Jews, these include Abraham, Moses, Elijah, David, and Solomon. Christians add to this list, Jesus, Mary, Peter, John the Baptist, John the Divine, and Paul of Tarsus. For Hindus, the key figures are Brahma, Lakshmi, Vishnu, Shiva, Durga, and so on. Then, beyond the pages of their sacred books, the history of each religion generates other important characters and episodes – the bodhisattvas of Mahayana Buddhism, the martyrs and missionaries of Christianity, the Hejira of Islam, and the Jewish "Mourning for Jerusalem," for instance. For present purposes, the significance of these elementary facts about the world's religions is this. Stories can be told in pictures as well as words. The episodes that they comprise, and the individuals who appear in them can be visually depicted as well as linguistically described. This being the case, religious belief and visual art very easily form a relationship.

Though the Bible is a literary text without any original illustrations, its stories and characters have proved a major stimulus to visual artists and their patrons. Indeed, probably the single largest category of religious visual art is of this kind, and it is certainly very ancient. The earliest icon, tradition holds, was the Holy Theotokis – St Luke's portrait of the mother of Jesus. Tradition aside, early Christian paintings are to be found in the Catacombs of Rome. They date from about 200 CE. While many of these wall paintings are simple symbols, there are also figures and "abbreviated" scenes from the Bible. Among them, it is easy to identify the "Good Shepherd," the "Resurrection of Jesus," the "Sacrifice of Isaac," "Noah and the Ark," "Moses striking the Rock", and "Daniel in the lion's den." The earliest surviving Christian church is located in modern Syria. It dates from 230 to 256 CE, roughly, and contains frescos of biblical scenes. A series of small statues dating from much the same period tells the story of Jonah. Early Christian marble sarcophagi were decorated with biblical scenes worked in high relief. New Testament miracles and scenes from Christ's Passion were commonly chosen for these sculptural depictions.

A similar history can be recounted for the visual art of Buddhism and Hinduism. The Ajanta Caves in the Indian state of Maharashtra date from the 2nd century BCE. They are decorated with paintings and sculptures of the Buddha, and depictions of episodes from the "Jataka Tales," an extensive body of literature about the previous lives of the

Buddha. Ancient paintings in the Mysore tradition of South Indian classical art depict Hindu gods and goddesses, along with scenes from Hindu
mythology.

These are all straightforward examples of how visual art can be used to
teach and to propagate religious beliefs – about events in the Bible, Hindu
mythology, or the life of the Buddha. At the same time, visual art stands
in a special relationship to the texts it illustrates. Though its assistance
in expounding their message has been widely valued, it has rarely, possibly never, been thought that religious pictures could replace sacred texts,
or even be an adequate substitute for them. Some of the most strikingly
beautiful religious art, in fact, is to be found side by side with these texts in
the form of accompanying illustration. What this suggests is that the distinctive contribution of visual art to religious belief should not be thought
of as the non-literary *equivalent* of linguistic texts, but an *enhancement*
of those texts. What might lend visual art this power to enhance sacred
text?

One interesting and important possibility lies in the ability of painters
(and sculptors) to determine how the things they choose to depict will
be seen by anyone who looks at their work. At a strictly material level,
every *painting* is nothing more than differently coloured pigments spread
in patches on a flat surface. As a *picture*, of course, it is much more
than this, and so the "art" of the painter may be said to lie in a mastery
of several important techniques that are employed in getting the viewer
to go beyond the two-dimensional expanse of pigment, and see three-
dimensional things within it.

The pre-supposition about representation and painting that came
under scrutiny in the earlier part of this chapter rests upon the fact that
one of the most obvious ways to do this is "representation." In representative art, perhaps the most basic power the artist exercises is choice of
subject. We see, say, a face, a flower, or a hillside "in" the picture, only
because the painter has chosen to put them there. They owe their *perceptual* existence, however, to more than this. Choosing a subject would not
amount to much without the use of composition, perspective, color, and
so on. It is by means of these techniques that the pigment on the surface
is turned into the object "in" the picture. Composition determines what
is central and what is peripheral; perspective determines how the objects
depicted stand in relation to each other; the use of color is key to making
"light" appear to fall on some objects, while leaving other objects in
"shadow." All these are ways in which those who look at the painting are
not merely allowed, but *obliged* to go beyond the observation of pigment

on a flat surface to the apprehension of perceptual objects – in a still life, a landscape, a portrait, and so on. And if, as is the case with abstract and "action" painting, there are only patches of color and geometrical patterns to be seen, that is not something that arises from the viewer's preference for pigments on canvas, but the choice of the artist, on whom the arrangement and relative vibrancy of the patches of color also depend.

Since these observations apply to all painting (and with some modifications can be extended to sculpture), they show how religious painters are able not only to incorporate the actions, occurrences, and characters that comprise the central affirmations of their religion within their paintings, but how they can also get us to see them in a certain way. Indeed, we can say more than this. Since there are no visual records (and often could be no such records), in order to visualize the people and events of their faith, believers and potential believers are reliant on the skills and imagination of painters (and sculptors). Yet more importantly, since the artist directs the believer's attention in certain ways, religious visual art can offer the devotee a means of spiritual orientation.

This distinctively religious use of visual representation can be made especially evident by comparing and contrasting paintings from one of the most famous periods of Christian visual art, Renaissance to Baroque (roughly 1450–1650 CE). The greatest religious artists from the early to the late Renaissance, especially in Italy, painted in what we might call a "heavenly" rather than an "earthly" style. That is to say, their pictures present the faithful with images of both biblical scenes and Christian saints whose effect is to give them an aura that sets them at a spiritual distance from ordinary life. The most obvious manifestation of this "aura" is the use of halos, which is to say, brightly colored circles that surround the head of the subject. In a group of otherwise recognizably human beings, this circle of light picks out the holy person or people on whom the artist wants us to focus. The halo is a symbol, but a similar effect can be achieved without the use of explicit symbols. The holiness of some figures in contrast to others can be realized by giving them unnaturally calm, untroubled postures and faces, even under conditions of great physical pain. Thus, in "The Stoning of Stephen" by Paolo Ucello (c. 1397–1475), St. Stephen's head is surrounded by a halo, but no less tellingly, his eyes are cast heavenward, and his unearthly spirituality is revealed by his kneeling unperturbed in the midst of an angry mob. The mob is hurling stones down on top of him, but his response is dramatically different to the more obviously human posture of an ordinary victim who would be cringing fearfully, fruitlessly guarding face and body against such painful blows.

The same "heavenly" kind of image is to be found in a painting of the *Martyrdom of Saint Sebastian* by Carlo Crivelli (1430–94). Despite being strapped to a tree, and shot through with no fewer than twenty-four arrows, the saint stands calmly looking up to heaven with a silver halo behind/on top of his head. The message is plain. Only someone who, thanks to the infusion of heavenly grace, has become truly indifferent to material misfortune could adopt such a posture. We need not suppose that either Ucello or Crivelli thought they were recording the actual attitude of St. Stephen or St. Sebastian in the face of martyrdom, any more than they thought that saintly people generally go about with halos. The point, rather, is to give striking visual representation to a contrast between the holiness of the saints and the brutality of unredeemed humanity.

The Martyrdom of Saint Sebastian is also the subject of a picture by the painter many consider to be the greatest of the "mannerists" – El Greco (1541–1614). In his distinctively stylized depictions of holy figures – Christ, St. Peter, St. Paul, the Virgin Mary, and so on – El Greco dispenses with halos, but succeeds in giving his figures an unearthly appearance nonetheless. This "otherworldly" character is conveyed by flowing costumes, indefinite lines, and flashes of light, but especially in the fact that they generally direct their eyes heavenward, or turn their faces humbly downward, giving them what might nowadays be thought of as a too obviously "saintly" look. This is clearly intentional. El Greco's beautiful painting of a boy blowing on an ember to light a candle, shows that he can turn his mastery of color and composition to entirely naturalistic ends. Unlike the images of Paul or Peter, the boy with the ember is definitely one of us. We may properly infer, therefore, that El Greco's "saintly" pictures have a special purpose. They seek to point viewers away from the everyday world that they *do* as a matter of fact inhabit, and toward a transcendent spiritual world they *hope* to inhabit, a world in which the saints now live, and to which devout Christians aspire. Though El Greco's religious paintings are highly distinctive, they are like many of his predecessors in this respect; they are visually *aspirational*. Their role, in other words, is not merely to depict the spiritual realm, but to encourage the faithful to seek it.

Mannerist paintings of this kind contrast sharply with the new realism of the early Baroque, a contemporaneous movement in painting that was brought to near perfection by the Italian painter Michelangelo Merisi da Caravaggio (1571–1610). Caravaggio, a younger contemporary of El Greco, is no less accomplished as a painter, and many of the works that he produced in the course of his short and turbulent career were commissioned by churches or church dignitaries. Some of them are still to be found in the original sanctuaries and side chapels where they were installed for expressly devotional purposes. Yet they are unmistakeably different from El Greco's. Carvaggio's depictions of saints and biblical scenes are highly realistic. Indeed, in their day they were criticized precisely for their realism. Those who were accustomed to idealized portraits of the saints thought that they ought not to be shown with dirty feet or heavily wrinkled faces. Once more, this is, it seems, a deliberate choice on Caravaggio's part. Some of his other paintings – *Cupid*, or the *Boy with a Basket of Fruit* – show that he could also idealize human and natural forms, though generally in a very sensuously physical way. The devotional relevance of his religious pictures, accordingly, can be said to be *inspirational* rather than aspirational. That is to say, whereas El Greco's figures convey an unearthly spirituality to which the believer is encouraged to aspire, Caravaggio's pictures show their saints as possessed of a humanity with which the worshipper is able to identify. Since the scenes in which they appear are unmistakeably biblical, this identification enables the worshipper to glimpse a spiritual dimension within, rather than beyond, the world of ordinary experience. Moreover, by this means the viewer is confronted with choices and not simply contrasts. This difference is specially marked if we compare Caravaggio's *Crucifixion of St. Peter* with El Greco's *Martyrdom of Saint Sebastian*. Like Crivelli, El Greco shows Sebastian alone and apart; his tormentors, though present, do not appear in either picture. Though tied up and pierced by a great many arrows, he remains composed, looking to the heavenly places for his comfort and salvation. Caravaggio's depiction of St. Peter's crucifixion places him right in the middle of three executioners who are painted with no less detail and attention than the saint. As these figures strenuously haul Peter into the upside down position in which (tradition holds) he was crucified, Peter looks at his own hand through which a large nail has been driven. His face is the only one we see, but it is neither placid nor composed, but expresses at one and the same moment, physical suffering and spiritual struggle. Viewers can thus see their reality and potentiality as human beings reflected in both the unredeemed executioners and their saintly victim.

A similar effect is achieved in a different way in the *Madonna di Loreto*. In this picture, which still hangs in the Church of San Agostino in Rome, Caravaggio has given Mary a delicate halo, but instead of gazing heavenward, or even at the holy child in her arms, she is looking intently and gently into the eyes of two praying pilgrims. The "ordinariness" of the pilgrims is striking – muddy feet, rough hands, crumpled clothing – but the composition of the picture ensures that, despite her haloed beauty, the holy Madonna is a real object for the pilgrims' prayers. Once again, as with the depiction of St. Peter, viewers are enabled to find spiritual inspiration in a world with which they can identify.

To summarize: along with feeling and the will, religious life engages the intellect. We often think of this in terms of the theological doctrines or philosophical theses that scholars, teachers, and prophets expound and that are contained in books, creeds, and confessions. But the full range of religious belief includes much more than this. All religions invoke stories, incidents, and characters that are related in their sacred books and recorded in their history. Since religious beliefs of this kind are rather less arcane, they are generally more widely propagated by and between the protagonists of a religion, and they have proved to be a major stimulus to both painters and sculptors. The visual artist, though, is not a mere illustrator of texts. Even beautiful work incorporated directly into a sacred text is referred to as "illumination" rather than illustration, signalling perhaps, that its role is to bring additional light and not merely provide exemplars. The role of the visual artist, then, may be said to go beyond recording or depicting, and to be an act of formative imagination in its own right. This formative power derives from the fact that the techniques they master in the service of imagination put special means into the hands of artists. It is by these means that artists can direct the minds of those who view their works. As the title of a famous book by the art critic John Berger suggests, the visual artist is a purveyor of "ways of seeing." And as the comparison of El Greco and Caravaggio has shown, these ways of seeing can incorporate differing spiritual orientations. Since visual images direct our minds in the apprehension of the subjects they present to us, this is no less true when those subjects are objects of religious belief.

Start

Visual Expression

A previous section distinguished three aspects of religious life – intellect, emotion, and action. The ability of visual artists to direct the mind and thus enable us to "apprehend" the spiritual significance of things, accords with the first of these. By means of visual imagination, the intellect is led to engage with religious narratives and characters, to understand them better and appreciate them more deeply. The underlying thought – that art has an important role to play in moral and religious "instruction" – was a commonplace in the seventeenth and eighteenth centuries. In the course of the nineteenth century, however, it became widely held that art has a more immediate connection with feeling. Accordingly, the most obvious connection between art and religion came to be seen to lie in the second of these three aspects of religious life, namely emotion. On this way of thinking, art, including visual art, is an essentially expressive medium. The artist does give a pigment-covered surface visual content, so that distinguishable objects can be seen within it. But the *ultimate* purpose of doing so is to be found at a deeper level, beyond depiction or representation, in the feeling or emotion that the painting embodies. Art, on this view, is really about expressing and communicating emotion.

The conception of art as the expression of emotion has had many distinguished advocates. Among the most notable are the Russian novelist Leo Tolstoy (1828–1910), the Italian philosopher Benedetto Croce (1866–1952), and the British philosopher and historian R. G. Collingwood (1889–1943).[4] Aesthetic expressionism is usually presented as a philosophical theory that applies to all the arts, though as we saw in the previous chapter, it has been invoked with special enthusiasm in application to music. While it has less frequently been explored directly in connection with visual art, it is nevertheless within the visual arts that "Expressionism" names a distinctive school of painting, one that arose, partly, in reaction to the more widely celebrated school known as "Impressionism."

The label "Impressionist" includes many famous artists, of whom Monet, Renoir, Cezanne, and Degas are perhaps the best known. The "Expressionists" include some very famous figures as well – Gauguin, Van Gogh, Kandinsky, Klee. All these painters were gifted individuals with distinctive approaches and accomplishments, so that neither "school" should be thought to have a uniform style, still less a unified aesthetic theory that informs all the works that may rightly be classified under these general labels. Even so, it is possible to identify some broad similarities and differences that are directly relevant to the topic of this section.

In the divergence from "realistic" resemblance characteristic of their paintings, the Impressionists sought to capture perceptual experience more adequately. While remaining committed to figurative subject matter taken from life, they abandoned precision of representation in the interests of capturing and conveying the way in which light affects color and thus influences perception. The mental habit of identifying things by bringing them under concepts means that we often do not much attend

---

4 For a fuller discussion of Croce and Collingwood see Gordon Graham, 'Expressivism: Croce and Collingwood' in *The Routledge Companion to Aesthetics* 3rd edition, edited by Berys Gaut and Dominic McIver Lopes (London and New York: Routledge, 2013)

to the individuality of perception itself. We just see "a tree," for instance, rather than this particular tree in this particular light. An important aim of the Impressionists was to capture accurately things as objects of visual perception. Thus, Claude Monet's picture of trains in the station at *Gare St-Lazare* (1877) gets us to pay attention to the visual effects of smoke, steam, and light, and to dissuade us from looking past these in order to identify the objects as railway engines. Impressionists, then, may be said to be concerned primarily with visual experience, and their interest in it was sometimes, and not entirely wrongly, called "scientific." It is a consequence of this "scientific" interest in the visual, combined with their concentration on objects and scenes from modern life, that the Impressionists produced no paintings obviously identifiable as "religious."

The Expressionist reaction to Impressionism lay in a preference for emotional impact over perceptual experience. The difference is strikingly embodied in the life and work of Paul Gauguin (1848–1903), who may be said to have moved from Impressionism to Expressionism. As a well-to-do stockbroker, Gauguin could afford to assemble a collection of valuable paintings. So for a time he collected Impressionist paintings, and as a gifted amateur painter, attempted some pictures in that style himself. However, his failure to exhibit successfully in an Impressionist exhibition in 1886 led him to turn in other directions. From this point on he sought his chosen subjects in lives and contexts much less "modern" and more rural than those of Parisian urban life. Having turned his attention away from the urbane, his use of color, appropriately, became much bolder. Significantly, his first major painting in the new style had a religious theme – *Vision after the Sermon: Jacob Wrestling with the Angel* (1888), the first of a series of religious paintings of which *The Yellow Christ* (1889) is the best known. Gauguin was personally acquainted with his contemporary Vincent van Gogh (with whom famously he quarrelled) and Van Gogh was quite explicit in his commitment to Expressionism. Referring to his picture *Night Café in Arles* (1888) – a subject also painted by Gauguin in the same year – Van Gogh wrote, "I have tried to express with red and green the terrible passions of human nature."

The aim of the Impressionists to capture visual perception in visual art is philosophically unproblematic. Depiction, so to speak, mirrors perception. But Van Gogh's declaration prompts this question. Can *emotion* be visually depicted? The answer, perhaps a little surprisingly, is "Yes." Emotion is not a visual phenomenon certainly, but this does not constitute the restriction that it might seem to. That is because there can be visual representations of the non-visual. Famously, the psychologist and film theorist Rudolf Arnheim used an example from the early days of film to make just this point. In Josef von Sternberg's movie, *The Docks of New York*, the "noise" of gunshot was given highly effective *visual* representation by the sudden rise of a flock of birds. No one watching this *silent* film could nevertheless fail to identify this visual representation with a specific sound. This example serves to show quite clearly that sounds can be represented visually. Accordingly, and notwithstanding a natural pre-supposition to the contrary, we must acknowledge that purely visual representation can go beyond the visual. The point to emphasize, however, is that sound and sight are indeed radically different senses, with different kinds of natural object for which we have different words – "the audible" and "the visible." Yet, as Arnheim's example shows, *representation* can convert one sense experience into another. This is what makes it possible for the audible to *become* visible in painting and film. In a similar fashion, the sense of touch can be represented visually. The tangible becomes visible when, for instance, artists successfully capture the "feel" of fur or fabric in their pictures.

These conversions of the audible, and the tangible, into the visual are sometimes known as "aesthetic synaesthesia." Synaesthesia properly so called is a psychological condition in which the stimulation of one sense (e.g. sight) prompts a sensation in another sense (e.g. hearing). It is most commonly observed at a certain stage of human development, and seems to be more likely in women than men. The scientific definition, observation, and explanation of synaesthesia are complex neurological matters with which progress has only relatively recently been made. But the concept of "aesthetic synaesthesia" (if not always known by that name) has been around much longer, and it need not involve any of these neurological complexities. It can be restricted, as it usually is, to relatively unproblematic cases of simple association.[5]

Some associations depend upon the contingent experiences of individuals. Someone may associate the smell of flowers with churches, say, because that is where the smell of flowers has most often been encountered. Someone else, with a different experience, would not make this association. But there are also a great many associations that people *commonly* make, associations that philosophers have sometimes called "natural signs." By means of these natural signs a strictly visual medium

---

[5] Nicholas Wolterstorff discusses the phenomenon and aesthetic significance of synaesthesia at length in Part III Chapter 2 of *Art in Action*.

can successfully be used to depict something non-visual. The concept of "aesthetic synaesthesia" names a general phenomenon rather than a special psychological condition. It refers to the familiar fact that visual art can capture non-visual, including non-perceptual phenomena. Since shapes and colors are perceptual phenomena, while sadness and happiness are not, it is easy to assume that there is an unbridgeable ontological gap between them. Yet, as simple drawings of a "happy face" or a "sad face" demonstrate, emotion can be visually depicted without any great difficulty. The widespread and rapidly increasing employment of the tiny digital images called "emojis" to add emotional nuance to text messages is evidence of just how intuitively intelligible a very large number of relatively simple images can be. Some of these – like the yellow smiley face – are modern examples of natural signs, but others – the stylized red heart for instance – are cultural constructs whose meaning is easily and quickly learned.

More sophisticated artworks can depict emotions more subtly than this. They can also depict more complex combinations of emotion, often by depicting human faces and gestures. "More subtlety" does not mean "more realist resemblance," however. Just like a simple monochrome "happy face," Edvard Munch's *The Scream* (1895) is made up of black lines on a white background. Yet it is easily identified as a powerful depiction of depression. While his pictures of *Despair* (1892) and *Anxiety* (1894) do use color, the figures in them do not look very much like human beings. Even so, the appropriateness of their titles is obvious. As with the examples from El Greco and Caravaggio, this is a deliberate artistic choice. Munch's *Girl Kindling a Stove* (1883) shows that lifelike resemblance is well within his painterly competence.

Munch's *Despair* and *Anxiety* illustrate another important fact – that colors often have natural emotional associations. It is because of this that the word "blue" can describe both a color and a mood. Similarly, "seeing red" commonly means getting angry, and a cowardly person is often described as "yellow." Van Gogh's claim about red, green, and the terrible passions of human nature is rather more ambitious than simply the exploitation of natural associations. His paintings are especially renowned for the surprising way in which the strong colors he uses seem to infuse flowers, landscapes, and furnished rooms with emotional overtones. In this respect, Van Gogh may be said to have started out on a path along which others went even further. The label "abstract expressionism," though once confined to a particular group of New York artists, has come to mean a style of painting that abandons the

figurative entirely and relies exclusively on the emotional content of
color alone. The paintings of Mark Rothko (1903–1970) are amongst
the most famous of these. Unlike Munch, Rothko left the colors to speak
for themselves, and did not make explicit such links as he may have seen
between his paintings and specific emotional states, giving most of them
numbers rather than titles, or simply naming them "Untitled."

While abstract expressionist painters may not always have been successful, their attempt to depict emotion non-figuratively is not in principle
absurd. The possibility is of special interest in the present context, because
if purely visual art can convey emotion, then it could in principle convey
religious emotion. If so, this is one way in which it could be expected to
serve religious life, and that is what some painters have hoped. Amongst
those who may be classified "abstract expressionists" the most intentionally "spiritual" was Wassily Kandinsky. In addition to his paintings,
Kandinsky published a short book on the subject. It is expressly entitled
Concerning the Spiritual in Art, and in a section headed "the language
of form and colour" Kandinsky tells us that the starting point for a
properly artistic spirit is "the study of colour and its effects on men."[6]
There follows an analysis of the ways in which colors can be altered and
blended to evoke different "feelings." Kandinsky claims that there are
some feelings so fine grained that words can at best gesture toward them
(a claim about visual art strikingly similar to Mendelssohn's claim about
music referred to in Chapter 2). It is on this observation that Kandinsky bases his belief in the spiritual power of painting, because, unlike
words, color has the potential to express and evoke these fine grained
feelings.

Suppose we grant this connection between the visual and the spiritual.
Is this "spiritual" in a religious sense? Are recognizably religious emotions to be included among the feelings that visual art can express and
convey? The answer to that question depends on the identification of
religious emotions. There can be disagreement about this, no doubt, but
it seems plausible to start by listing joy, grief, exhilaration, and anxiety.
All these emotional states figure in religious life and are the subjects
of religious reflection. The problem is that they figure in non-religious
life also. So what emotions, if any, should we identify as *distinctively*
religious? There are three, broadly speaking, to which writers on religion
consistently refer. The first is religious awe, a strange mixture of fear and

---

[6] Wassily Kandinsky, *Concerning the Spiritual in Art* (New York: George Wittenborn, 1977)
p. 36

attraction that a sense of the sacred or the numinous seems to generate.[7] Awe describes a religious mentality that is both drawn to, and unnerved by, the holy, as Moses was to the Burning Bush in the book of Genesis. A second distinctively religious emotion results from a sense of human vulnerability. We are conscious, as no other animal is, of our contingency and mortality, and this gives rise to a distinctive form of anxiety. The third, also peculiar to human beings (though certainly not shared by all of them), is a sense of guilt, sin, or unworthiness. This emotion arises from the fact that we have the capacity to consider our actual lives in the light of certain ideals – of beauty, integrity, and moral excellence. If we do, then an awareness of how far we fall short of these ideals can powerfully oppress us. As an old expression has it, we *labor* under a sense of sin. For simplicity's sake, I shall name these three emotions "wonder," "anxiety," and "sinfulness." This enables us to frame the question in which we are interested. Can wonder, anxiety, and sinfulness be given purely visual expression?

Since as we have seen, emotion in general can be visually depicted, the obvious answer might appear to be "yes." But it confronts this problem. For a very wide range of cases, the proper identification of an emotion – what emotion it is – depends upon the object to which it is directed. Let us agree with R. G. Collingwood that anyone in an emotional state undergoes a "psychical disturbance," a feeling of some kind, and it is this *felt* aspect of emotion that distinguishes it from thought. Now it is easy to suppose that this "feeling" is the emotion itself, until we notice that, even though a feeling can have a specific character (depressing, agitating, elating), this is often not sufficient to tell us what emotion it is. For instance, a "depressed" feeling is common to grief, to loneliness, and to disappointment. Feeling "agitated" is common to anger, to frustration, and to fearfulness, while feeling "elated" is a "psychical disturbance" common to pleasure, joy, and excitement. Thus while feeling is certainly an indispensable component of emotion, what makes a specific emotion the emotion it is lies in its connection with something *other than* feeling. Generally speaking, this is a state of affairs that is *both* the originating cause *and* the mental object of the feeling. So, for instance, grief is a depressed feeling that is *caused by* and *directed at* loss; frustration is agitation *caused by* and *directed at* failure; excitement is exhilaration *caused by* and *directed at* success, and so on.

---

[7] The most famous exponent of this concept was Rudolf Otto in *The Idea of the Holy*, trans. John W. Harvey (Oxford: Oxford University Press, 1923).

Emotions, then, need objects as well as feelings. These objects are not themselves felt, but apprehended by thought. Without this intellectual component, the feeling is largely indeterminate. Indeed, it is a sign of defective feeling – clinical depression and mania, for instance – that an alternation between "high" and "low" feelings takes place without any identifiable causing object. Clinical depression arises *without* bad things happening, mania arrives even when there is nothing to be elated about. When emotions have *proper* objects the feelings that are part of them become intelligible – something that can be understood. People correctly described as grieving, for instance, must not only experience a feeling of sadness, but recognize that it is caused by the death of a loved one. The same "blue" feeling prompted by the loss of a cell phone, say, though it might be very powerful, even incapacitating, would not be grief. High excitement at winning a lottery is intelligible both to the winner and third parties. The same degree of elation at losing the lottery would be unintelligible.

It follows from this that when instances of religious emotions like wonder, vulnerability, and sinfulness are correctly described as such, we have to be able to identify a proper object as their cause. Let us say that "awe" names a feeling that someone truly experiences, but if it is caused by and directed at, say, the accomplishments of a sporting hero, it is not the religious emotion of wonder. Similarly, "gloom" let us say, is the name of a negative feeling, but if it is caused by and directed at, for instance, my having indulged my love of chocolate, then it is not the religious emotion of sinfulness. We should conclude, then, that religious emotions must be caused by and directed to a properly religious object. We may now restate the question. Visual art is able to stimulate feelings, but can it direct them in such a way that we have reason to identify those feelings as components of religious emotion?

We observed earlier that figurative painting (including symbolic representation) can direct the mind, and if now we add to this the observation that shapes and colors have the power to express and convey emotion, it is not hard to see how (at least in principle), visual art could serve the expression and communication of *religious* emotion. The use of form and color, as the expressionists claimed, can stimulate feeling. Figuration directs this feeling to an identifiably religious object. It does not matter whether the figuration is realistic, surreal, or symbolic. Any of these can enable the mind to identify and direct the accompanying feeling.

This possibility is demonstrated by comparing Francisco de Zurbaran's painting *Agnus Dei*, with Paul Klee's *The Lamb*. The former, painted in several versions between 1635 and 1640, is a highly lifelike painting of a young sheep tied by the legs and (the picture invites us to assume) awaiting slaughter. The colors in de Zurbaran's picture are muted – browns and blacks mostly. These are "gloomy" colors but the negative feeling of pity is prompted principally by representational resemblance. This feeling is then directed to a properly religious object by means of the title – *Angus Dei* – the name given to Jesus Christ in the Bible. The picture thereby converts a feeling of pity into a devotional attitude. By contrast, Klee's picture, painted in 1920, is not at all lifelike. Its lamb is almost a cartoon, with very vibrant colors. The heightened feeling the picture invokes, to which we cannot easily give a name, is directed to the same religious object as de Zurbaran's, not in this case by a generic title "Lamb," but by pictorial content – a cross, positioned like a spike through the head of the lamb with blood dripping from it. Both pictures evoke and direct feeling. This feeling is identifiable as religious emotion because the pictures, in different ways, direct it toward the sacrifice of Christ. That is what makes them emotionally powerful from a religious point of view. Without its identifying title, though, while we might well find de Zurbaran's picture disturbing, the emotion would be pity for the sufferings of an animal. So too, relying only on the *title* of Klee's – *The Lamb* – we have no reason to think of the Lamb *of God*. It is the symbolic visual content that directs us to this special object. In either case, without these identifiers – the one linguistic, the other figurative – we would have no reason to regard the pictures as *religious* art.

Many commentators have supposed that the religious or spiritual content of abstract expressionism can be experienced *without* any specifically religious identifiers. The theologian David Brown, for instance, says that the paintings of Kandinsky and Klee show a "pre-occupation with form and colour as means of highlighting the underlying divine reality of the world," while in Rothko's "implicitly religious canvases one senses a tragic longing for transcendence,"[8] a longing we could think of as something rather close to what I have called "anxiety." But can we make this connection with any confidence? Klee's expressionist *Lamb* can be set alongside Zurbaran's *Angus Dei* since for all their obvious differences, it is no less *explicitly* religious. The cross and the blood provide the additional elements needed for the feeling to be properly directed. Without such evident pointers, determining the mark of the *implicitly* religious

---

[8] David Brown, *God and Enchantment of Place* (Oxford: Oxford University Press, 2004) pp. 136–7

feeling is problematic, because we cannot tell how it differs from *non-religious* feeling.

The Rothko Chapel project in Houston Texas provides a good illustration of this. Though it was not completed until a year or so after Rothko's suicide, it was a commission to him and built in accordance with his conception of how it should be. On completion it was filled exclusively with fourteen of his paintings. These are all large color field works in very dark hues, the kind of painting that became Rothko's trademark. Some tourists visiting the Rothko Chapel may experience complete indifference, but most people, it seems plausible to suppose, can be expected to experience a feeling of some sort. They are likely, however, to be feelings of many different kinds, including awe, admiration, and pleasure, but also, perhaps, contempt for the paintings, or confusion about them. These too are "feelings" that the paintings prompt. By calling the building a "chapel," however, it is implied that some of these "feelings" are more appropriate than others – pleasure rather than contempt, for instance. – and that between simple pleasure and outright contempt, there are some feelings that are *properly* called "religious." This supposition is confirmed by the fact that the Rothko Chapel guidebook describes the building as "a holy place open to all religions." It then it adds, though, "and belonging to none," thereby immediately raising this question. If the "chapel" belongs to *no* religion, what reason is there to think that the feelings the paintings in it arouse are, or have to be, *religious*? Leaving pleasure and contempt aside, why wouldn't other *kinds* of feeling be equally appropriate? Rothko himself declared at one point that he was interested "only in expressing basic human emotions – tragedy, ecstasy, doom, and so on." In ordinary speech these words often have religious overtones (though one might wonder if "tragedy" is properly called an emotion). Let us grant that the emotions Rothko names are at least quasi-religious. There is nevertheless good reason to ask why *these* terms are the appropriate ones. On what grounds do we determine that a large patch of brilliant color expresses emotional "ecstasy," rather than describing it more simply as visually "thrilling." Why should we say that a large patch of dark color expresses "doom," rather than saying it makes us feel depressed? There seems to be nothing in pure color that compels us to connect it, as Brown does, with "a tragic longing for transcendence"? Generalizing on this point, we can agree that colors stimulate feelings, while denying that there is any reason for us to be more specific. Why is it not enough, in describing our reaction to them, to stick with generic "feelings" – pleasure, depression, sadness, excitement – and refuse to settle on any of the wide variety of emotions that have these feelings in common?

To summarize: This section has been concerned with the ways in which visual art can serve the emotional dimension of religious life. It is a commonplace, though not uncontentious, that art in general is in some way intimately related to the expression of emotion. The art movement known as Expressionism is of special interest in this connection because it shows how, despite departing quite radically from figuration, color and form can be said to retain emotional expressive power. The question that this raises, nevertheless, is whether and to what extent, this fact makes it possible for purely visual art to express and convey identifiably *religious* emotions. If, as seems plausible, psychical feeling is an essential component of all emotion, it still remains the case that emotions properly so called are more than psychical feeling. In order for them to be identified as the emotions they are – sorrow and not just gloom, joy and not just elation – they must be caused by, and directed at, appropriate objects – the death of a child, the restoration of a friendship. Figurative painting can depict just such objects, and by means of color and form diffuse them with feeling. Painting at its most abstract abandons all such objects. Sometimes it has done this in pursuit of "pure" feeling, and the idea of pure, thought-free feeling has had a special allure for visual artists in the modern period. Yet, however impressive the resulting paintings and sculptures may be, the cost of abstract expression is a loss of specificity. Sorrow, guilt, depression, anxiety, are all merged into gloom, while success, surprise, joy, are all merged into elation. The intelligible differentiation of psychic feeling requires identifying markers. Consequently, for works of visual art to be expressions of religious emotion, they must incorporate recognizable signs of properly religious objects. In other words, visual expression without visual identity remains religiously indeterminate.

Visual Identity

The indeterminacy of visual art need not be taken as a criticism. Indeed, one way of characterizing abstract art is to see in it a deliberate, self-conscious determination to avoid all forms of identification, both linguistic and visual. The American artist Jackson Pollock (1912–56) became famous for his "action" paintings – pictures created by pouring and splashing color on large canvases. Pollock's "method" emphasized speed and spontaneity so that no preconceived idea, even on the part of the painter, would be allowed to influence the outcome. If we "see" anything

in Pollock's action paintings, it is a consequence of the arbitrary imposition or association of images on the part of the viewer. While his early
works did have figurative elements and titles – *Going West* (1934–5) for
instance – as his paintings became more abstract, he abandoned titles as
well as figuration. A few are given nondescript titles such as *Mural* (1943)
or *Pattern* (1945), but for the most part, like Rothko's, Pollock's paintings
are expressly labelled "untitled" or just given a number. This is a notable
feature of other abstract expressionists. Mondrian, as he moved away
from the figurative, produced "compositions," and Kandinsky produced
numbered "improvisations."

The aim, it seems evident, is to go as far as possible along the trajectory
begun by the Impressionists. By excluding everything that might deflect
us from the purely visual, we are compelled to focus on perceptual experience itself. According to the great art historian E. H. Gombrich, Pollock
drew inspiration from Chinese calligraphy and Zen Buddhism, and perhaps like other abstract expressionists he saw painting as a vehicle for
mystical experience. "Kandinsky, Klee and Mondrian were mystics who
wanted to break through the veil of appearances to a higher truth .... It
is part of the doctrine of Zen (though not the most important part) that
no one who has not been shocked out of his rational habits of thought
can become enlightened."[9] Gombrich may be correct in seeing in abstract
expressionism an aspiration to forge a connection with mystical experience. If the arguments of the previous section are correct, however, at most
this "experience" consists in a "psychical disturbance" of a very indeterminate kind, so indeterminate in fact that it could not bear out the distinction Gombrich makes between "veil of appearances" and "higher truth,"
though it is just such a distinction that religious mysticism requires. On
the contrary, regardless of what the artists themselves may have thought, it
seems most plausible to interpret abstract expressionism as the presentation of *nothing but* appearance. It should be added immediately, that this
need not diminish our estimation of the abstract expressionists' achievement. Their paintings have been widely acclaimed, and rightly so. Still,
the justificatory basis for such acclamation can satisfactorily rely on their
remarkable ability to reveal the astonishing beauty and wonder of the
visual in itself without appealing to anything more mysterious. Instead of
taking us *beyond* the veil of appearance, they give us occasion to delight
in it. We do not need to attribute a "mystical" character to them in order
to ground our admiration, and this is just as well, since if the analysis of

---

[9] E. H. Gombrich, *The Story of Art* 16th edition (London: Phaidon Press, 1995) p. 604

this section is correct, there does not seem to be any very good reason to make such an attribution.

These remarks about the intrinsic interest and value of the strictly visual apply most obviously to non-figurative art. At the same time, the striking differences of style that set "modern" art off from its classical precursors transcend the figurative/non-figurative division. "Modern" art includes both. This is easily illustrated by our earlier example. Paul Klee's *The Lamb* and De Zurbaran's *Agnus Dei* are both figurative paintings. Yet the visual differences between them are not only evident, but striking. In this respect, a comparison between these two pictures provides an illuminating example of a trajectory from the seventeenth century to the nineteenth that is replicated in many recognizably Christian pictures. When the trajectory is extended even further in time, however, the question of continuity becomes problematic.

This is most easily illustrated by considering a long sequence of paintings with the same subject. Several important subjects recur again and again in Christian painting. One, for obvious reasons, is the Crucifixion. There are hundreds, probably thousands, of renderings of this scene by notable painters and sculptors. Antonello de Messina (c.1430–1479) painted several versions in the mid-fifteenth century, and 500 years later, Marc Chagall (1887–1985) did just the same. No one could fail to see radical visual differences between them, but even so, and without the title, Chagall's *White Crucifixion* of 1938 recognizably has the same subject as Messina's *Crucifixion* of 1455.

The same point is not nearly so obvious when we consider another recurrent subject – the "The Annunciation." This is the traditional name for the occasion recorded in Luke's Gospel when a very youthful Mary is visited by an angel who tells her that she will become pregnant by the Holy Spirit. The scene of their encounter has been painted by at least one great master, often several times over, in every century from the thirteenth to the nineteenth. The list includes – Giotto (1267–1337), Botticelli (1445–1510), Leonardo (1452–1519), Titian (1485–1576), El Greco (1541–1614), Caravaggio (1571–1610), Rubens (1577–1640), Murillo (1617–82), Goya (1746–1828), Rossetti (1828–82), and Tissot (1856–1902). The same episode continues to inspire as, for instance, in the series of studies painted by the Romanian artist Sorin Dumitrescu (b. 1946). This impressively long list captures a story of both continuity and change. Continuity lies in the fact that "The Annunciation" has been a subject popular with painters across 800 years; change lies in the fact that the styles in which they have painted it have altered greatly. In every

century from Giotto to Dumitrescu, it is easy to identify both the same
scene and a very different style.

So dramatic are some of these changes in style that an important question naturally arises. How much change in style can there be without a
change in subject? Even if we agree – as the previous section argued –
that figuration is essential for the feeling evoked by a work of art to be
converted meaningfully into a religious emotion, it is evident from the
examples cited that commitment to figuration is compatible with immense
stylistic variation.

We might think of this variation in the following way. Each artist
(or each period perhaps) offers its own a distinctive "take" on the
Annunciation. By painting the subject differently, it presents a new visual
interpretation of it, and thus enables Christians (and others) to apprehend
the biblical event afresh. This seems a plausible way to relate content
and style, continuity and change. However, it raises a further issue. At
what point does *variation* become *deviation*? That is to say, how much
"interpretation" is possible before the thing "interpreted" is transformed
into a different subject?

Modern paintings of the Annunciation, in fact, provide some examples that raise just this question. The depictions of the artists listed above,
though considerably different, do not differ nearly as drastically as a few
paintings with this title produced in the twentieth century. Three are especially notable – *Annunciation* by the Cubist Fernand Leger (1881–1955),
Annunciation by the surrealist Rene Magritte (1898–1967), and *Annunciation Study I* by the abstract expressionist Brice Marden (b. 1938). Leger's
picture has the face of a woman to whom a dove seems to be murmuring.
Is the dove intended to take the place of the angel? Perhaps so, and if so,
then we might ask about the significance of the substitution, though it is
hard to see how we could distinguish between substitution and abandonment; a dove is not an angel. Magritte's is also a figurative painting, with
rocks, trees, clouds, and sky. But in the positions traditionally occupied
by Mary and the angel, we find three motifs that turn up repeatedly in
Magritte's work – a curtain of iron with bell-like shapes, a piece of paper
cut into patterns, and two "bilboquets" (to use Magritte's term), i.e. sil-
very white balusters. This picture is not an abstract. On the contrary, it
exhibits Magritte's quite remarkable facility for representational art, the
motifs mark it with his distinctive style, and his choice of title is deliberate.
But what relationship does it have – could it have? – with the scene from
Luke's Gospel? Marden's *Annunciation. Study 1* is an abstract – eight
black and white lines of varying thickness on a white background. This

is, possibly, even further removed from the Gospel story than Magritte's. The fact that Marden entitled it "Annunciation" may lead us to suppose that there must be *some* connection. That does not mean that we are, or will ever be, in a position to uncover it. For most people, I imagine, the gap between Luke's story and Marden's picture is just too great to see any link at all.

Some people will be tempted to reply that we should not expect any strictly *visual* connection. Rather, the choice of title in all three cases alerts us to the fact that each artist is expressing in painting his *emotional* response to the story of the Annunciation. What we should be looking for in the picture is an expression of the artist's emotion, and its possible awakening in us. Now it is to be noted immediately that this familiar response rests on a biographical claim that is assumed to be true, but hardly ever documented in fact. We do not know what emotional response, if any, Leger, Magritte, or Marden experienced when they heard the Gospel story, if indeed they ever heard it. Nor do we know anything about their state of mind as they painted these pictures. That is a very telling point against many versions of aesthetic expressionism. However, it is not the major point to be made here. Suppose that in some way the emotional response of these painters is indeed embodied in each of the paintings. Suppose, furthermore, that we can tell what that emotion is. This information would still not be sufficient to determine the identity of any of them as a religious painting. This is for the very obvious reason that the emotion to which they gave, and meant to give, expression may not be an appropriately religious emotion. Perhaps Leger, Magritte, or Marden hoped to give visual expression to their contempt or loathing for a story they regarded as a fanciful imposition of established religion, or a despicable idealization of submissiveness in women. Their success in expressing contempt through the medium of visual art, and our ability to identify it in this way, would still not warrant anyone classifying the picture as a religious one.

The uncertainty works both ways of course. If we can't be sure whether these cubist, surrealist, and abstract paintings are indeed paintings of "The Annunciation" we can no more attribute negative than positive attitudes to them. But actually, even when images are more determinate, uncertainty can arise for a different reason. Returning to the subject of the Crucifixion provides us with a famous example. *Immersion (Piss Christ)* is a work by the American photographer and artist Andres Serrano (b. 1950). The work is a red-tinged photograph of a crucifix submerged in a glass container of what the artist claimed to be his own urine. The figurative content of the image is unmistakeably Christian, and in 1987 the work won the annual "Awards in the Visual Arts" competition sponsored by the Southeastern Center for Contemporary Art. The adverse reaction it provoked in many quarters, however, was precisely because its use of a Christian image was *unmistakeable*. It was used, its critics alleged, not to stimulate feelings of veneration in the presence of Christ's sacrificial death, but to prompt contempt and ridicule. Serrano's rather beautiful photograph, then, can be taken in different ways. To regard it as simply visual, makes it irreligious. To regard it as the crucified Christ dropped into urine makes it anti-religious. To regard it, as some commentators did, as a visual expression of the low place that Christ has come to occupy in modern society, arguably recovers a measure of religious significance, but more by way of sociological commentary than religious devotion. The main point to be made here, however, is that none of these interpretations is any more defensible than any other. We can interpret *Immersion* in whichever way we please.

Art Versus Iconography

It is important to note with respect to this particular example, that demands for the piece to be banned from public exhibitions, on the grounds of its offensiveness to Christians, met with protests from those who wanted to protect artistic freedom from religious censorship. This assertion of the importance of artistic freedom against deep-seated religious sensibilities reveals some of the potential tension between art and religion whose emergence was discussed in Chapter 1. The tension arose, it will be recalled, from the aspiration to artistic autonomy that came with the idea of art's intrinsic value, an aspiration expressed in the slogan "art for art's sake." The quest for creative autonomy motivated many artists to throw off what they had come to see as the *constraints* of religious and political patronage. This is one reason why art and artists were increasingly seen, and saw themselves, as politically subversive, a role for the arts that some Marxists expressly advocated.

In the case of religion, however, freedom from ecclesiastical patronage did not, in itself, imply a wholesale rejection of religion. The effect was more subtle than that. The autonomy of art as a practice demanded artistic integrity on the part of the painter, and this led to the transformation rather than the abandonment of religious painting. Religious subjects lost their authority as the determining focus of artistic endeavor. They no longer circumscribed the work of the artist. Instead, they became vehicles through which painters and sculptors strove to realize their artistic individuality, and to express their spiritual insights. Thus, whereas the aim of Giotto, say, in painting his *Annunciation* was to put his skills at the service of the Gospel story, the aim of Magritte was to make the story (or at least its title) a means by which he could give further expression to his unique style of painting and his subscription to surrealism. The concern of those who resisted opposition to *Immersion (piss Christ)* was to protect Serrano's freedom as expressed through his artistic individuality. In this way the high value placed on artistic integrity, and the importance this lent to individuality, meant that the visual markers of religious identity – stories, events and characters from the Bible, and history of the Church – became materials like paint and stone, and thus subservient to the personality of the painter and sculptor. In short, religious meaning gave way to artistic expression, even where what the artist "expressed" could with some plausibility be thought to be the fruit of mystical experience or spiritualized emotion. Experiencing a personal response was then extended to viewers also, who were invited to find in the work a spiritual or emotional "meaning" of their own.

This historical trajectory – from authoritative religious depiction intended to inform and inspire, to authentic artistic expression aiming to engender a "felt" response on the part of the viewer – characterizes the development of religious visual art in the Christian West. It contrasts sharply, however, with the story of visual art in Eastern Orthodoxy. The split between Eastern and Western Christianity, at times acrimonious, is usually dated from the Great Schism of 1054. In reality, this formal rupture simply marked the culmination of differences and divisions that had grown up over a long period of time. As was noted at the outset of this chapter, roughly two and a half centuries earlier, a great debate about the use of icons had taken place. On the one side were the "iconoclasts" who wanted to be rid of icons lest they foster idolatry, and on the other the "iconodules" who greatly valued icons as means of intensifying religious devotion. Eventually, the iconodules won the debate, and icons became an established part of Christianity in the East. But the developing role of visual art in Orthodoxy followed a quite separate path to the way in which Western Christian art developed.

The result is a deep difference between the two, easily detected by considering again our earlier example – pictures of *The Annunciation*. As we saw, for a very long time this biblical episode has proved an artistic stimulus to Western European painters. Over several centuries, as we might expect, the style of paintings produced with "Annunciation" as their title changed dramatically, so dramatically, in fact, that the only point of connection between the fourteenth and the twentieth centuries – Giotto's *Annunciation* and Marden's, for example – seems to be the title. The same subject has been no less popular with iconographers, who have produced beautiful icons of *The Annunciation* over an even longer period. However, while a comparison of icons from the thirteenth century with those of the twenty-first does reveal some perceptible differences, these are minor in comparison to the differences between Western paintings from the same periods. The most obvious and surprising fact about icons is just how *little* change there has been over 800 years. Set alongside the history of literature, music, architecture, and sculpture, the astonishing continuity that is to be found in the visual art of the icon far surpasses that of any other artistic form.

Why is this? The answer is not to be found in the enforcement of standards by some external regulatory authority. The continuity is sustained by the practice of icon making itself, within which the relationship between artist and work functions quite differently to the way the contemporary art world normally thinks of it. Strictly, icons are not painted; they are "written," and while the "school" of iconography within which the icon "writer" is working may be important, the individual "writer" is very rarely identified (The venerated Russian iconographer Andrei Rublev (c.1360–1430) is a notable exception). This anonymity is a reflection of the fact that the iconographer's treatment of the subject is not the "free play of the imagination" around which the Kantian aesthetic is constructed. Indeed, it is not determined by the imagination of the artist at all. Rather, icon writing begins with the choice of a traditional template in accordance with which the artist works. This template establishes from the outset just how the subject is going to be treated. Furthermore, the methods employed in making the icon – the preparation of the wooden surface, the mixing of colors, the application of gold – are all highly circumscribed. There are right and wrong ways of completing these stages. Importantly, these methods are inextricably linked with spiritual exercises by which the artistic endeavor is accompanied. Icons, in other words, are at the farthest possible remove from, for instance, Pollock's action pictures. Similarly, the individuality of style that is so striking in, say, Magritte, has no equivalent in the icon. It is plausible to think that in contemporary Christian visual art of the West, the role of the work is to give expression to the spiritual sensibility or experience of the artist. On the basis of personal "feeling," the painter or sculptor brings a distinctive "interpretation" to the subject. Precisely the reverse is true of Orthodox icons. The spirituality of the icon writer is shaped and intensified through the discipline of creating the work. The individuality of the artist is submerged in the religious icon that he or she produces. Submersion is not the same as suppression. Skilled iconographers strive to avoid icons that are simply copies of what went before. The novelty of an icon, nevertheless, lies in finding a fresh continuity with the old. Consequently, the emphasis is not to do something interestingly different, but to realize as fully as possible the religious identity that is embodied in the icon.

This difference further explains the contrasting role of visual art in the two religious traditions. At one time, Christian paintings informed and taught the faithful. They have largely lost that function, and insofar as they have any function in the practice of religion, it is to be a source of contemplative inspiration – something like the glimpse "beyond the veil" that Gombrich attributed to Pollock and Rothko, a visual intimation of a less material world. Insofar as paintings do serve this function, however, they are as likely to serve it in an art museum as in a church. Icons, by contrast, have their proper home in churches where they are expressly installed with appropriate ceremony. Their acknowledged purpose is to serve as a focus for prayer, often within the context of the liturgy. Icons are created to be beautiful, certainly, but they are not there to be admired for their beauty. The beauty that the iconographer's artistry has given them has a higher purpose, namely both shaping and channelling religious veneration. It is worth recalling that the iconophiles were as anxious about idolatry as the iconoclasts. Taking their cue from John of Damascus, however, they argued that the worshipper's veneration is not directed at a beautiful image (as an aesthete's might be said to be in the gallery of an art museum), but at the properly holy person, object, or event represented in the icon – *Christ Pantocrator* (Ruler of All), *Holy Theotokis* (Mother of God), *The Annunciation, The Transfiguration*, and so on. Since holy things are eternal and unchanging, so the images that focus this veneration will be largely unchanging also. That is why what they require is the discipline of a template, not the free imagination of the artist. In this way, whereas the art of the religious painter serves his or her particular spiritual or emotional experience, the art of the iconographer is placed entirely at the service of the icon as a focus of prayer and veneration.

The fact that icons are *used* by worshippers, and not merely contemplated, shows how visual art can engage directly with religious practice. In so doing, it connects intellect, emotion and will with an identifiably religious object. An icon of *Christ Pantocrator*, for instance, has two different facial expressions, thereby incorporating a religious affirmation – the humanity and divinity of Christ. The fingers of the ascended Christ, ruler of all things, are raised in blessing, thereby directing the spiritual longing of the individual to a source of blessing. It is this combination of affirmation and emotion that makes the icon a special focus for the individual's activity of prayer and veneration in the course of the liturgy.

The advertised purpose of this chapter was to explore an important dichotomy of opinion about visual art and religion – the belief that they have a natural affinity, and the no less widely held belief that they are in some ways at odds. We might express the issue this way. Is art an ally in venerating the beauty of holiness, or does it constitute an alternative ideal and invite us to venerate the holiness of beauty? Icons are a fine example of the first possibility, though by no means the only one, while the aspiration to artistic autonomy and integrity that has gradually become dominant in European "high" art since the eighteenth century, is a clear example of the second.

A Footnote on Film

There is one form of visual art that has been mentioned fleetingly in the course of this chapter and about which something more needs to be said – namely the art of film. Modern film is not a purely visual art of course. It usually includes drama, dialogue, and sound effects as well as moving visual images and is in many respects the *Gesamtkunstwerk*, or synthesis of the arts, that Richard Wagner imagined opera could be. For this reason, it does not fit neatly into the divisions around which the chapters of this book are organized.

Still, it is not hard to find films from the earliest days of cinema that have religious themes. Throughout his career as a director, Cecil B. DeMille (1881–1959), widely acknowledged as a founding figure in the Hollywood film industry, made movies based on the Bible. *The Ten Commandments*, released in 1923 was the first of a biblical trilogy, being followed by *King of Kings* (1927), and *The Sign of the Cross* (1932). In 1949 he made another biblical movie, the highly acclaimed *Samson and Delilah*, and in 1956 concluded his long and productive career as a director with a remake of *The Ten Commandments*, a film that fifty years later was still listed in the top ten best epics ever.

Cinema in other parts of the world also took up religious themes at an early stage. The silent French film *The Passion of Joan of Arc* (1928) by the Danish director Carl Theodore Dreyer is a much celebrated example.

Still further afield, just one year later, the Indian Prabhat Film Company produced a silent movie with a Hindu theme – *Gopal Krishna* (Child Krishna) directed by V. Shantaram. Over the years since then, a number of celebrated directors, leading actors, and commercial film companies have worked on films with religious themes. The work of the famous Swedish director Ingmar Bergman (1918–2007) includes a "Trilogy of Faith" consisting of the films *Through a Glass Darkly* (1961), *Winter Light* (1963), and *The Silence* (1963). In 1965, on a much grander scale, United Artists released *The Greatest Story Ever Told*, an American epic film with a star-studded cast, produced and directed by George Stevens, who had won an Oscar in 1956 for *Giant*. This enormously expensive (and lengthy) film was not the success that Stevens hoped, and for a time "big" religious films became less common. The opening decades of the twenty-first century, however, witnessed their return, perhaps because of the astonishing success of Mel Gibson's *The Passion of the Christ*, released in 2004. Gibson's film recounted the closing narrative of the Christian Gospels very closely, but used reconstructed Aramaic, vernacular Hebrew, and Latin for the dialogue (with English subtitles). Contrary to many people's expectations, it was a major commercial hit, becoming the highest grossing religious film and the highest grossing non-English-language film of all time. While *The Passion of the Christ* did not meet with universal critical acclaim, Xavier Beauvois' *Des Hommes et Des Dieux* (*Of Gods and Men*), which tells the story of the kidnap and assassination of Trappist monks during the Algerian War, showed that films with religious themes can be highly successful on both counts. Premiered at the 2010 Cannes Film Festival, it won the Grand Prix, the Lumières Award, and the César Award 2011. It was also a box office success in France, the United Kingdom, and the United States of America.

Many religious films have been of a very poor artistic quality, but these examples show that films with religious themes, often made by distinguished directors, can be both commercial and critical successes. What is uncertain, however, in the relationship between recognizably religious movies and the practice of religion. First, we might wonder if there is not an inevitable tension between entertainment and worship. This is not to say that worship has to be dull, but rather that part of the aim of entertainment is *distraction*, and distraction provides relaxation precisely because it relieves our minds of the pressure of serious concerns. Religion, by contrast, is quintessentially concerned with serious matters. This sense of tension between religion and entertainment, though, is not confined to religious cinema. The same concern led some people to question Handel's great oratorio *Messiah* on its first appearance. Handel's work was a musical setting of a "wordbook" sent to him by the librettist Charles Jennens. The wordbook consisted entirely in sentences from the Bible, skillfully arranged, and amended slightly here and there. Jennens's hope in sending it, was that once allied to Handel's operatic gifts, the biblical story of Jesus would reach new hearers by being taken out of a church setting and presented as "an entertainment." It was this very ambition, however, to which contemporary critics especially in England, objected. They thought the idea of being "entertained" by Christ's Crucifixion was deeply misconceived. Perhaps in this case we can say that history proved them wrong, but whatever the truth about this particular example, the critics had some basis for their reservations. Any attempt to combine entertainment and devotion runs a double risk of going wrong. Either it will be too entertaining to stimulate any devotion, or it will be too serious to succeed in entertaining.

A second anxiety about religious films comes from the side of the film maker, and draws upon a different tension. Films that carry a "message," and aim to push people toward faith, fall into the category of propaganda rather than art. A plausible example of just this is Harold Cronk's *God's Not Dead* (2014) in which a committed Christian student successfully resists the skeptical intellectual onslaught of his atheist philosophy professor. This was a sufficiently great commercial success to warrant the product of *God's Not Dead 2*. But in large part its success lay in its appeal to church based audiences, who, there is reason to think, favored it not as an example of the filmmaker's art, but because they saw it as a powerful weapon in the battle with atheism. And insofar as they were entertained, it was because they enjoyed the "goodie" beating the "baddie." *God's Not Dead* made use of film, not as an art form with its own integrity, but as an instrument that would serve to bolster religious faith in a skeptical culture. This is not any worse than any other form of advertising or promotion, but it explains why the film failed to win any critical accolades, even though Cronk had previously demonstrated his artistic gifts by winning an award at the Beverly Hills Film Festival for his earlier short film *The War Prayer* (2005).

There remain, of course, many fine films that cannot be dismissed as either "mere" entertainment or religious propaganda. The film review website *Rotten Tomatoes* said that "*Of Gods and Men* asks deep, profound questions that will linger in the audience's mind long after the movie." Anyone who has seen the film will agree that this is a very plausible claim to make about it. It is one that could be made about innumerable films, however. Moreover, while the questions that linger after such films can often be connected with distinctively religious concepts such as faithfulness, sacrifice, penitence, forgiveness, redemption, and so on, it is to be remarked that these concepts are often applicable to films that are not explicitly, still less avowedly religious.

Still, even when an avowedly religious film successfully avoids the charge of propaganda, and leads the mind of the audience to ponder on deep questions about the human condition, it does not seem right to say that watching the film is itself a religious activity. Of course, the lingering thoughts it prompts might subsequently lead some members of the audience to pursue some sort of religious activity. But it need not do so, and the key point is this. If a film has no such outcome, this is not in any way a failure on the part of the film maker. Nor has the audience's appreciation gone astray if it does not prompt them to prayer or worship.

At their best, it seems, religious films are properly described as thought provoking. They can also be moving. In terms of the threefold distinction employed in this chapter, then, they connect with two dimensions that are an important part of religious consciousness – intellect and emotion. But they do not have any direct connection with will or action. By the nature of case, moviegoers are largely passive spectators. They are not invited to any action in the way that, for instance, a hymn, a church building, a devotional poem, an icon, or a procession, invites those who appreciate them properly to action. When movies are intended to elicit our agreement with a religious doctrine, or stir us to participate in religious worship and prayer (or confirm us in the activity in which we already participate), they do so at the cost of relinquishing their status as art. They become, in other words, a mode of preaching. Preaching, as we will see in the next chapter, does have an artistic dimension, but as might be expected, its more obvious connection is with the literary arts.

4

Literature and Liturgy

It was observed early in the previous chapter that every major world religion has some form of scripture, some book that the adherents of the religion think to be of special value and significance. These books differ in character; some are histories, others are books of law, others poetry and myth. As Chapter 3 also noted, they differ in the authority that believers attribute to them. The three great "Religions of the Book" – Judaism, Christianity, and Islam – think of their scriptures as divine revelation, while in the religions of the Far East even highly revered texts are not always regarded in this way. The role that these books play in religious practice also differs, since some are used in worship and others are not. But the fact that *texts* have this special place inevitably gives the literary arts greater prominence in most religions than the other arts. As we have seen, some religious traditions are wary of painting and sculpture, while others are no less wary of architecture. Even music, which is found in almost all religions, does not have the same status as text. There are no musical equivalents to "canonical" writings.

Not all religious writing, of course, is an exercise in literary art. In the medieval period (and at other times) Christian theology was classified as a "science," and many theological works clearly favor logical rigor and conceptual system over elegant or memorable expression. It is also true that many religions have lent considerable importance to recording their own history, and in this case (theoretically at least) fact and accuracy take first place. Both hagiography and apologetics are common, certainly, but there are also many serious and sustained attempts by believers to know their own history. This variety in types of writing is not confined to ancillary or peripheral religious texts. They can be found within a single holy book. The Hebrew Bible, for instance, contains theological exposition (in *Proverbs*), and historical narrative (in *Kings* and *Samuel*) alongside the poetry of the *Psalms* and imaginative stories such as those of *Jonah*, *Job*, and *Daniel*.

It is true that the distinctions between science, history, and literature are not always easy to apply. Indeed, whether some parts of the Christian Bible – the creation stories in *Genesis*, and the miracle stories in the Gospels, for instance – are historical or not, and whether this matters, has often been a subject of intense and sometimes very heated debate. Happily, it is a topic that we need to touch on in detail at only one point. That is because, even if the distinction between historical writing and literary art is somehow crucial, it remains the case that the religious importance of a text need not depend upon its historicity. Take for instance, the parables of Jesus. The Prodigal Son and the Good Samaritan are two of the most famous stories ever told. There is nothing to suggest that in telling them Jesus was recounting actual events, and if, as everyone seems to agree, these are indeed fictions, it is nonetheless plain that they are meant to be both illuminating and instructive. This immediately raises one issue that has occupied philosophers of literature – how can *fiction* teach us anything? That is the first topic with which this chapter will be concerned.

Religious stories that aim to teach lessons are not confined to scripture. Nor indeed, are they confined to fiction. Historical stories of saints and martyrs are also meant to instruct and inspire. The existence of such stories is a reminder that the "literature" of most religions goes far beyond their scriptures. Furthermore, this much larger body of literature often provides materials for worship and devotion – prayers, chants, hymns, devotional poetry, and the like. Literature of this kind is marked, very often, by its striving for linguistic beauty, and by its use of literary devices – meter, rhyming, alliteration, metaphor, allegory, and so on. Here we encounter another question that philosophers of literature have asked. What does poetry add to prose? This is a succinct, if somewhat artificial, way of raising a broader philosophical issue – what contribution does intentionally *literary* expression make to the meaning and substance of what is said?

Even when we have answered this question, there is a further matter to be considered. Religions *use* words. That is to say, beautifully expressed prayers are not merely there to be read, but to be *said*. Religious poems set to music are intended to be sung. It is common for scriptural passages and other important religious texts to be read aloud (as at a Jewish or Christian service) or recited in public (as the Quran is). In short, religious words are most often encountered in religious activity. But what is the point of such activity? What makes religious actions intelligible? What reason do human beings have to engage in them? This question raises some basic issues in the philosophy of action, and these will constitute the third concern of this chapter.

Truth and Fiction

Is the creation story in *Genesis* history, or is it a myth? Did Jesus really rise from the dead, or did his disciples imagine it? These have seemed to many people not merely real questions, but crucial to the credibility to the Christian religion. From this point of view, re-classifying the story of Creation or Resurrection as "poetry" has been regarded by both Christians and skeptics as a misguided, and fruitless, attempt to dodge or fudge the issue. Scientists who think that the theory of evolution has rendered the first chapters of *Genesis* redundant, and creationists who reject the theory of evolution because it conflicts with *Genesis*, are fiercely opposed to each other. Yet on one point they make the very same assumption – that the value and significance of these Bible stories stands or falls with their "literal" truth. But what exactly is *literal* truth? If, for a moment, we leave behind the vexed case of religious belief, we will see that this concept is not as straightforward as it has often been thought to be.

Here is a short story.

A hungry fox went into a vineyard where there were fine ripe grapes. Unfortunately for him, the grapes were growing on a trellis so high up that he was not able to reach them. 'Oh well, never mind!' said the fox. 'Anyone can have them for all I care. They are sure to be sour'.

This is one of Aesop's many fables and it has a "moral," namely, that people often claim not to have wanted things once it turns out they cannot have them. This moral, let us agree, states a truth about human beings, but how does Aesop's story bear it out? To begin with, it is clearly imaginary, and even fanciful. The episode it recounts never happened; foxes don't eat grapes, and they cannot speak. The moral appears to be a truth about experience, but since the story is both fiction and fantasy it does not and could not be based on observation. Aesop has not discovered, but invented the supporting evidence for the moral he wants to press. Besides, even if, *per impossibile*, he had actually experienced the event he recounts, there remain two serious doubts. Why should we suppose that the behavior of foxes tells us anything about human beings? Even if it did, generalizing from one episode is not a genuine piece of induction.

There is something very odd about these criticisms. It is not that they are themselves false. As a matter of fact, they are all true; foxes *don't* eat grapes or talk, and have a quite different nature to human beings. Yet, for all that, anyone who voiced these criticisms *seriously* would reveal a deep misunderstanding of what story telling is about. There is something to be learned from the fable. That is the sense in which it conveys a truth. The irrelevance of the criticisms results from a failure to see that the moral of a fable is not a fact or explanation that requires, or even lends itself to scientific investigation and empirical evidence. Truth in fiction is not that kind of truth.

What has gone wrong? The truth in fiction is being tested inappropriately. The tests the "critic" employs implicitly, and illicitly, apply certain familiar dichotomies – fact *versus* fiction, observation *versus* imagination, illustration *versus* evidence. The mistake lies in the assumption that these dichotomies are logically relevant regardless of context, whereas, on the contrary, context is essential in determining their relevance – or lack of it. Consider the "observation *versus* imagination" dichotomy. There is one obvious context – anticipating the future – in which this dichotomy is plainly irrelevant, because it cannot be applied meaningfully. Suppose someone has predicted that the morning traffic will ease by 9 a.m. It may be important for me to know whether this is a realistic or a fanciful prediction. Since it relates to the future, however, observation is impossible. I cannot *see* how things *will be*. Of course, I can *imagine* how they will be, but this is of no help because I can as easily imagine the traffic snarled up as flowing freely. The crucial distinction – "realistic *versus* fanciful" – does not map on the "observation *versus* imagination" distinction. We need to be realists in our beliefs about the future, but however we are to do this, direct observation cannot be the answer.

This has an important implication for the subject of this chapter. "Realistic *versus* fanciful" is also a distinction that can be applied to fiction. Accordingly, it is not always the "fact *versus* fiction" distinction that should interest us. Some works of fiction are realistic, while others are fanciful. To describe them as "fanciful" need not be a criticism. Fanciful stories can be very entertaining, and sometimes the more fanciful the better. J. K. Rowling's Harry Potter series were fantasy not realism, but their enormous commercial success testifies to their huge appeal as entertainment. From realist fiction, however, we generally expect to get something more than entertainment. Our hope is that we will *learn* something. Yet, whatever we may learn, and by whatever means we learn it, it remains fiction. Realism in this context means "truthful" or "true to life," but that never turns fiction into fact. The conclusion to be drawn is this. If we want to grasp the idea of truth in literature, we should not simplemindedly apply the fact/fiction dichotomy.

Consider now the "illustration *versus* evidence" dichotomy. The *Second Book of Samuel* recounts a story about King David and the prophet Nathan. David's lustful eye had fallen on Bathsheba, the beautiful wife of Uriah the Hittite. Desiring Bathsheba for himself, David arranged to have Uriah sent to the most dangerous position in the battle with the Ammonites for the city of Rabbah. His plan worked. Uriah was killed, and David was able to marry Bathsheba. Some while later, Nathan the prophet, sent by God, enters the king's presence and tells him a story about a rich man and a poor man. Nathan recounts how a traveller called on the rich man, but being too mean to provide a sheep from his own flock to feed his guest, the rich man seized the one ewe lamb that the poor man possessed, and used that to feed the stranger and thereby fulfil his duty of hospitality. David takes Nathan to be reporting a recent incident. He furiously demands that the rich man be brought before him and forced to make generous restitution for his heartless selfishness. In a famously dramatic moment, Nathan replies, "*You* are the man!"

For present purposes it is pertinent to note that contrary to David's initial assumption, Nathan has imagined the episode he recounts, and David, crucially, does not figure directly in the story. Nevertheless, it is not hard to see, just as David himself comes to see, that it somehow refers to him. His own immoral conduct with respect to Uriah and Bathsheba is being brought in evidence against him. Nathan's imaginary story, in other words, compels David to see the reality of what he, David, has done. Assembling evidence is often a rational strategy in arriving at a verdict, but imagination, this example shows, can be another means by which reality is brought home to us.

Jesus' parable of the Good Samaritan illustrates the same point. He tells it in the course of a discussion, and in response to a question. The discussion relates to the scope of the ethical principle "Love your neighbour as yourself," and Jesus is responding to the legalistic question "Who is my neighbour?" The parable that follows recalls an incident on the road to Jericho when a traveller is attacked and robbed. As he lies injured, two professional holy men, a priest and a Levite, come along the road in succession. Fearing the danger into which they might run by attending to the injured man, they pass by on the other side. Then a Samaritan (whom orthodox Jews would normally look down upon) comes by, stops, helps the victim, takes him to safety, and pays for his recovery. "Who" Jesus asks, "was neighbour to this injured man?" The question is rhetorical, of course, since it answers itself. The point to be made is that if, as Christians suppose, there is a truth to be learned from the story, it is a truth to which the fact/fiction distinction is irrelevant. That truth remains, whether the story of the Good Samaritan was the product of Jesus' imagination, or a recent event of which his audience was aware, and that he used to convey the same lesson.

These examples demonstrate the need to discriminate carefully between and within religious texts. Whatever truths they seek to convey, we should not expect to apply a "one size fits all" epistemology. At the same time, it is somewhat misleading to speak of different kinds of truth – "scientific truth" contrasted with "poetic" or "religious truth" for instance – because this easily raises, and feeds, the suspicion that the concept of a different kind of truth is invoked chiefly to fend off the rational criticism of cherished beliefs. Truth comes to us in different *ways*, we might say, but not in different *kinds*. Still, given the intractable disputes that the concept of truth so easily engenders, it is better, perhaps, to avoid the explicit use of the term, and refer instead to what there is to be learned from different kinds of writing. This enables us to explore the contrasting ways in which the human mind can be brought to apprehend important aspects of existence.

Reality and Imagination

It is reasonable to assume that works of systematic theology employ the same sort of logical and conceptual methods as philosophy, cosmology, and other theoretical inquiries. Similarly, there is every reason to think that the methods of religious history will involve much the same mix of empirical evidence and interpretation that political history requires.[1] So the central question here is how religious texts *as literature* could bring us to the apprehension of important religious truths. In the previous chapter we identified three distinctive religious emotions to which I gave the names "wonder," "anxiety," and "sinfulness." Emotions, it was argued, are not simply sensations like feeling hot, or cold or tired. They are

---

[1] With respect to the *Hadith*, Islam has developed a distinctively different method of authenticating stories about the life of the Prophet. It is not a historical method as practicing historians would understand this.

feelings directed at the object by which they are caused. Grief, for instance, is a feeling directed at the great personal loss by which it has been caused.

Religious emotions also have proper objects (or "objective correlatives" to use T. S. Eliot's terminology again). This is what makes them feelings that can be understood and not merely experienced. Just as someone's fearful feeling becomes intelligible once we know that it arises from the perception that he or she is in danger, so the intelligibility of these religious emotions rests on their being internal or subjective responses to external or objective conditions. We can usefully name "sacredness," "transience," and "wickedness" as the three "objective correlatives" of "wonder," "anxiety," and "sinfulness." A sense of sin is intelligible when it arises from an acknowledgment of wickedness, whether individual or collective. It is possible for people (children for instance) to be oppressed by a sense of sin and shame (cruelly induced by others, sometimes) when they have done nothing wrong. But we recognize this as a pathological condition. No one can *intelligibly* feel sinful while knowing themselves to be innocent. Similarly, though people can, for no particular reason, have a debilitating feeling of anxiety even amounting to feeling "doomed," such a feeling is made intelligible when the inescapable transience of life has suddenly been brought home to them, often by illness, accident, or the death of a loved one. So too, a feeling of awe or wonder is properly grounded when it arises in response to a perception of the sacredness of things.

Transience and wickedness are realities of the human condition, almost everyone will acknowledge. The reality of sacredness is the issue on which the irreligious and the religious, both theistic and humanistic, divide. The question "Is nothing sacred?" can express a confident rejection of an irreligious world, or a more diffident wistfulness. For the purposes of this chapter, I shall assume that sacredness is as much a reality as transience and wickedness. The assumption is warranted because the philosophical issue in which we are interested is not directly concerned with the existence of the sacred, but with how literary exercises of the imagination, no less than logical proofs and historical evidence, could be the means by which the mind is directed to realities of this kind.

The story of Nathan and David has already provided an example. Though fictional, the episode of the rich man/poor man is an image of *real* wickedness; it exhibits selfishness, ruthlessness, and cruelty. That is why David's initial supposition that Nathan is recounting an actual event is both understandable and at the same time inessential. Whether fact or fiction, the story captures the reality of wickedness. Of course the truth that Nathan (and God) intend David to learn and acknowledge is about his own wickedness in the matter of Uriah and Bathsheba. The punch line, "*You* are the man," draws a parallel that redirects David's moral outrage at the rich man onto himself. The resulting sense of sin realigns his emotion to the reality of his own conduct. It does so, however, only in virtue of a further imaginative act on his part. David does not observe the events Nathan recounts, and he is not offered a logical demonstration of the parallel Nathan intends him to see. Both are acts of imagination on his part. Because they bring about the same outcome as observation and proof would do in other circumstances, we can rightly employ *epistemological* terms, and talk of the *mind* being directed, lessons being *learned*, and the *reality* of the circumstances having been revealed.

Probably most people's initial thought is that David learns a *moral* lesson. This in itself implies nothing specifically religious. But a background supposition, which he and Nathan share, is that wickedness is an offense against the laws of God, the eternal laws of right and wrong. That is what makes it a religious and not just a moral lesson, and warrants the label "sense of sin." This is not a peculiarity of the Hebrew Bible. The Hindu scriptures have a corresponding concept of an eternal moral law – *karma* – which can never ultimately be evaded, and this is partly the lesson of the story in the Bhagavad Gita. The Gita is the best known part of the Mahabharata, an enormously long epic poem that runs to over a million lines. Another of its major themes is the transience or impermanence of human life. It recounts the story of a Pandava prince, Arjuna, a brilliant warrior engaged in battle. He finds himself filled with doubts, prompted by his realization that the enemies he is about to fight include his own relatives, some of his friends, and even the teachers he has previously revered. In search of guidance, he turns to his charioteer, who is also Lord Krishna, God Incarnate. The seventeen chapters that follow are lessons Krishna teaches Arjuna, about the deceitfulness of appearances, the eternal divine energy that creates, pervades, preserves, and destroys all things, and the wisdom of discerning the difference between sacred and profane. True wisdom and strength flow from living in accordance with the divine law by rejecting the wickedness of anger, lust, and so on. In teaching Arjuna these lessons Krishna draws on all the devices that characterize the literary arts – rhyming, meter, dialogue, parable, simile, and metaphor. Moreover, since the teaching takes place in the midst of a battlefield, the story itself, perhaps, is its own controlling metaphor.

An immense amount of interpretative attention has been given to the Bhagavad Gita and a great deal of philosophical reflection has been based on it, all on the assumption that there is much to be learned from it. The point to be emphasized here, however, is that it has all the marks of a literary work rather than an historical narrative or philosophical treatise. The lessons to be learned from it, furthermore, are not specific to Arjuna in the way that the lesson Nathan intended David to learn is. They are about the nature of human existence in general, and how it is to be lived. Partly, the Gita's purpose is to bring readers to an acknowledgment of the transience and moral confusion of the world in which they find themselves, and partly it aims to point to ways in which they can nevertheless orient themselves to this reality. As this implies, the lessons it teaches are not merely theoretical or philosophical; they are practical, concerned with how to live, given the way the world is and our nature within it. That is why several of the chapters are devoted to explaining and advocating varieties of yoga. At the same time, it is not merely action, but attitude that matters. Accordingly, other chapters elaborate on faith and detachment.

There is an inevitable openness about our response to texts like these. They may fail to convince, be blocked by delusion, met with denial, or manipulated by the wiles of self-deception. These possibilities, however, do not tell against literary writing as such, in religion or more broadly. People can and often do refuse to accept the clearest evidence – in courts of law or with respect to family history, for example – and they will sometimes fail to grasp the most rigorous logical or mathematical proof. But even when religious texts of a literary nature are successful in bringing someone to an acknowledgment of the reality of sacredness, transience, or wickedness, they can intelligibly awaken quite different attitudes, and lead to correspondingly different actions.

To begin with, as some of the examples in previous chapters have implied, an intense awareness of the sacred commonly results in two notably contrasting emotional responses. One is awe – a reverent stillness and attention to the presence of the sacred, the response encapsulated in the story of Moses, hiding his face before the burning bush, out of which the voice of God tells him to remove his sandals since he is standing on holy ground (*Exodus* 3). The other is ecstasy – a response whose most dramatic exemplar is to be found in the Sufi "whirling dervishes" of Turkey. Believing that "they are the ones whose hearts rejoice in remembering God" (*Quran* sura 13), the dervishes throw themselves into energetic dancing while repeating over and over phrases from the Quran expressly recommended by Muhammad for this purpose – "La ilaha illa'llah" (There is no God but God), and "al-hamdu li'llah" (Praise to God). Awe and ecstasy are very unalike, but they are both recognizable responses to "the holy."

Similarly, the consciousness of wickedness can also prompt importantly different reactions. For most, perhaps, a sense of sinfulness calls forth a quietly sorrowful and penitential spirit, giving voice to prayers of confession. But there are much more emotionally excessive expressions of penitence and lament. Physical self-flagellation has been a common practice over many centuries, both in Roman Catholicism and in Islam, and remains so in some places even to the present day. For instance, in a traditional flagellation ritual called "Talwar zani," Shi'ite devotees, usually young men, will use a chain with blades to beat themselves until they bleed. The object of their lament is their failure to have saved Husayn as God's appointed successor to Muhammad. Some devout Catholics still practice a (much milder) form of self-flagellation during personal prayer, using a whip made of knotted cords.

There is then, no single emotional response to the realities of existence to which the world's religions point. But it is also possible to acknowledge these as objective conditions without *any* properly religious response. Confronted by Nathan, David, for instance, could have acknowledged his own wickedness, and even seen it as sin, without thereby being brought to an attitude of repentance. Similarly, while someone could come away from reading and reflecting on the Gita fully convinced of the transience of things, and so adopt an attitude of detachment, taking up yogic practices as a means of attuning themselves to the divine, someone else, being no less fully convinced of the transience of things and fleeting nature of our lives, could be led to nihilistic despair or hedonistic indulgence (conflicting reactions that the Jewish *Book of Ecclesiastes* appears to commend in different places). Or, someone might meet the transience of human life with a kind of defiance, resolutely determined to rejoice in being "human, all too human" (the title of Friedrich Nietzsche's book of aphorisms). Nietzsche was influenced in his thinking by Schopenhauer, and shared both Schopenhauer's rejection of the Christian God and his admiration for the truths revealed in Eastern mysticism. At the same time, he expressly rejected Schopenhauer's pessimism and refused to accept that the only response to the transience and vulnerability of human life is ascetic withdrawal. Properly understood, Nietzsche thought, even the cruelty and ruthlessness of which human beings are capable can be a cause for celebration. The transience of human life and the brutality of human nature are realities that honesty and clear-sightedness oblige us to acknowledge. The properly human response, and the only self-respecting one, is to draw upon our own strictly psychological resources. In the absence of God (whose "death" Nietzsche announced in *The Gay Science*, published four years after *Human, all too Human*), these are the only resources we are left with by which to affirm the value of existence in the face of annihilation.

Despair and defiance do not exhaust the non-religious possibilities. There is also the attitude that Friedrich Schleiermacher called "extreme practicality," something Schleiermacher thought far more destructive of religion than philosophical skepticism. "Extreme practicality" is a cast of mind that is determined to focus on the limited concerns of daily life about which something consequential can be "done." From the point of view of what is "practical" in this sense, a religious response to life is too "mystical." "Despair," from the same point of view, verges on the pathological. For extreme practicality, "defiance" is the outcome of a self-indulgent "existential crisis" that may prove attractive to the philosophically minded, but it is not of any service to ordinary life. Far better then, just to get on with living.

The inevitable openness of religious texts means that they admit of both a variety of religious responses, and of none. There is one further possibility, namely isolating them from practical life by making them objects of academic study. The great writings of the world's religions can be admired and enjoyed from a purely literary and linguistic point of view. This is precisely the perspective within which they are generally regarded in the modern university. Concern about the potential conflict between academic inquiry and religious affiliation has led most scholars of religion to adopt an attitude of impartial neutrality to the texts about which they are expert. This deliberate difference of attitude can be marked by saying that academic study aims to treat the great religious books as ancient texts, not as holy writ, and to do so by treating them as cultural artefacts of particular times and places. There is undoubtedly something to be gained from this approach, and it is hard to deny that a great deal has been learned since the nineteenth century when avowedly "scientific" study of this kind began. At that time, many religious people perceived a threat to their faith in this important academic development, and feared that the authority of their scriptures would be undermined by linguistic analysis and historical "criticism." It is a debate that continues, but for present purposes it is enough to observe that many millions of people continue to regard the Hebrew Bible, the Old and New Testaments, the Quran, the Upanishads, the Adi Granth, and so on, as *holy* writ. Clearly, academic study has not put an end to that, and from this simple fact we may infer that, regarded as sacred writings, religious texts still have something else to offer besides a knowledge of ancient worlds. People who respond to these books as holy writ find in them, not only sources of revelatory insight and illumination, but the means by which their response to this revelation can be articulated.

More importantly perhaps, it is also true that the world's holy books have deeply shaped human responses to the realities those books themselves reveal. A religious attitude to the reality of existence contrasts with despair, defiance and "extreme practicality" in being characterized by prayer, meditation, worship, and praise. The great texts do not merely *prompt* these practices. They also *inform* them, because it is in religious literature that the language needed for these practices is to be found. That is our next topic.

Words and Worship

Not all holy writ is ancient. The Sikhs' sacred book, the Adi Granth, was elevated to the status of holy writ by Guru Gobind Singh, the tenth Sikh Guru, as recently as 1708. It nevertheless provides an especially clear example of the way in which sacred texts supply the language of worship. Now known as the Guru Granth Sahib, Sikhs regard their holy book as the sole and permanent successor to the ten Gurus who founded their religion. They believe that it contains within it a complete revelation of God, not just for them but for humanity, and that nothing in it may ever be changed or discarded. In addition to the religious teachings of the ten Gurus, the Guru Granth Sahib also includes a large number of hymns and poems written by them. These are recited and sung directly in Sikh worship in the presence of the holy book, a copy of which sits in an honored place in every gurdwara or temple, and is venerated like a Guru. For Sikhs these hymns and poems provide the only authentic language of worship.

Though Sikhism is a relatively modern religion, and a radical departure from the two great religions of India, Hinduism and Islam, its attitude to the Guru Granth Sahib displays an intense conservatism common to much older faiths. Many of the world's religions have a "sacred" language that their adherents are required to use exclusively for the practice of prayer and worship. Often this is a "dead" language such as Biblical Hebrew, Latin, Church Slavonic, or classical Arabic. Behind this conservatism lies a deep-seated concern to ensure that the purity of divine revelation does not become distorted by wilful human meddling, something that editing and translating can scarcely avoid. That is why, even when translations of the Guru Granth Sahib or the Quran are tolerated, they are never accorded any religious authority, or used in worship.

This is not true of all religions, however, and even when it is, their literature may still exceed those texts that are regarded as holy writ. This larger body of religious literature grows continuously, as new hymns, poems, histories, lives of saints and mystics, prayer books, and spiritual meditations are added to the vast number that already exist. Such ancillary works often draw very extensively on holy writ, translating, selecting, reordering, and paraphrasing its contents to compile other handbooks for religious practice, both individual and corporate.

An especially striking example is the Anglican *Book of Common Prayer* (BCP) which, until relatively recently, was used with very little variation by Anglican Christians in almost every part of the world. The first version of this book was compiled (over a ten-year period) by Thomas Cranmer, Archbishop of Canterbury under King Henry VIII (1491–1547). Cranmer drew on a wide variety of sources, both ancient and contemporary, translated everything into English, and added some new material. The result of his labors was published for the first time in 1549. It included forms of worship for morning prayer, evening prayer, and holy communion, liturgies for thanksgiving after birth, the baptism of infants, marriage, and burial of the dead, as well as ceremonies for ordaining priests and bishops. In all these services, the book makes very extensive use of bible texts and imagery, and it prescribes regular recitation of the entire Jewish psalter in English translation.

Over the next 100 years the *Book of Common Prayer* went through a number of relatively modest revisions. In 1662, a version was authorized that continued in use without significant change for a further 300 years. Meantime, an English version of the Christian Bible was produced by a royally appointed committee of scholars, who spent seven years translating the original Hebrew and Greek texts. Finally published in 1611, it became known as the King James Version (KJV) and remained the standard English translation for more than 200 years.

The BCP and KJV were radical innovations. Hitherto, the Christian Church in the West had had its own sacred language, Latin, and indeed, less than a century before they appeared, people had been imprisoned, and even executed, for attempting to translate the Bible into English. But both books were highly innovatory in another way as well, because when they were being composed, English was not a single uniform language. People in the regions of England spoke a number of equally well-established dialects, and many of Henry VIII's subjects in Scotland, Ireland, and Wales spoke no English at all. Consequently, if they were to succeed in producing a book of *common* prayer, and if this translation of the Bible was to be authorized for use by all, the authors and translators had to invent a "standard" English that would be intelligible to the speakers of different dialects.[2] The result was that the BCP and the KJV were written in a language that no one had ever actually spoken in daily life. The language in which they were written, however, soon came to be regarded as the way in which English *ought* to be spoken. Importantly, this normative role extended beyond the purely linguistic. Together these two books provided a norm for how God was to be addressed in English and how the rites of passage – birth, marriage, death – were to be regarded and celebrated. For many generations thereafter, the BCP and KJV provided people with a language for worship, a language which then came to shape and pervade the hymns, prayers, sermons, ceremonies, theological reflections, and religious experiences of English-speaking people, a category that grew enormously as Britain established colonies in North America, Asia, Australia, and Africa.

The literary beauty of the BCP and KJV has often been remarked upon. This is part of the explanation for their enduring appeal to Christian worshippers over many centuries. In this respect they reflect a common feature of religious language when it is not confined to an official "sacred" language. Liturgical worship, spiritual meditation, and the practice of prayer, in some way demand deliberately "literary" language; the prosaic will not serve. Even what appear to be freestyle forms of worship and completely extempore prayers in the language of everyday life, will often reveal on careful examination that they employ poetic devices extensively – assonance, alliteration, rhythm, figures of speech, repetition, cadences, and so on.[3] It is here that we can locate the basis for a close connection between religion and the literary arts.

Why does the practice of religion place a premium on poetic devices? A significant part of the answer undoubtedly lies in their practical value. Rhythmic and rhyming speech is easier to remember, alliteration and assonance assist in this, while metaphors and similes are more "catchy" and compelling. Rhythm also has the advantage of making it easier to coordinate groups of people saying the same thing. Another part of the answer, however, is closely related to an issue in the philosophy of literature, namely the distinctive nature of poetry.

Poetry is a linguistic art, and accordingly (leaving nonsense poetry aside) the meaning of a poem must derive from the meaning of the

---

[2] Martin Luther's translation of the Bible similarly required, and created, a standard version of German.

[3] This is especially notable in some American Protestant traditions.

language in which it is written. Now the same is obviously true of news-paper reports, legal transcripts, scientific papers, and business proposals. Yet the poetic use of language is evidently very different. To begin with, unlike ordinary prose, poetry is exceptionally hard to translate effectively from one language to another (sometimes impossible, it seems). Secondly, a poem can never be completely paraphrased as a newspaper report or a business proposal can. In this respect, poetry is again different from prose. What explains the difference? A key idea is the expressive perfec-tion for which poetry strives. The aim of a newspaper report, say, is to convey information effectively, and so long as the information is commu-nicated, the precise wording is not of any great significance. The aim of the lyric poet, on the other hand, is to capture a thought or a sentiment perfectly – which is to say, give it expression in a set of words that can-not be improved upon, and cannot be amended without significant loss. This striving for perfection may fail, of course, and everyone acknowl-edges that only some people have a sufficient poetic gift even to make the attempt. To the extent that they succeed, however, the poem ceases to be a personal expression, and becomes an ideal of thought and feeling which anyone might understand and contemplate.

This is not to say that the reader must *share* the thought or sentiment that the poem embodies. There are many poems that express a degree of romantic love, grief, or patriotic fervor far beyond anything that occurs in the course of most people's lives. Yet, even if I have never loved so passionately, or lost so devastatingly, I may nonetheless savor the artistic accomplishment in a poem that, as it were, speaks on behalf of those who have. I need not require or expect that it should speak to my own expe-rience. Consider, for example, the most impassioned love poems of the English "metaphysical" poet John Donne (1572–1631). Were most peo-ple to suggest to a spouse or partner that one of these poems expressed their own feeling, this would in all likelihood reflect either their emo-tional insincerity, or their conspicuous failure to appreciate Donne's poetry.

There is reason to think that as a young man Donne really was intensely passionate, but it is essential to emphasize that it is not necessary for the poet to have experience of these emotional "highs" either.[4] The greatest poetry is an imaginative achievement, not a biographical report. It would

---

[4] In acknowledgment of a potential patron, Donne wrote an emotionally powerful elegy on the death of a young girl that he barely knew.

be absurd to think, for instance, that Shakespeare had to experience all the jealousy, ambition, love, despair, remorse, paranoia, light heartedness, or grief that he powerfully depicts in the poetry of his plays. It is his astonishing, and seemingly unlimited power to give imaginative expression to these many states of mind *without* having experienced them, that constitutes his unsurpassed literary gift.

So too with religious poems and hymns. When ordinary worshippers sing some of the finest Christian hymns, for instance, the religious sentiments expressed often far exceed their own. They may also exceed the religious sentiments of those who wrote the hymns. Contrary to what is often supposed, and in contrast to the love poem example, this need not imply either insincerity or a lack of understanding. Religious worshippers set their sights on higher things, hoping to connect with something that transcends ordinary experience. Emotional elevation by means of hymns, poems, and prayers that imaginatively express *ideals* of feeling play an important part in this endeavor. Isaac Watts (1674–1748) composed a large number of beautiful lyrics. His hymn, "When I survey" is a meditation on the Crucifixion and a good example of idealized religious sentiment. It closes with the lines

> Were the whole realm of nature mine
> It were an offering far too small.
> Love so amazing, so divine
> Demands my life, my soul, my all!

We may safely suppose that the religious commitment of millions of Christians who have sung this hymn has fallen very far short of this heartfelt affirmation. But to suppose that for this reason they should never sing it, mistakes the hymn's role in worship. It is not an expression of how they feel (or how Isaac Watts felt, for that matter, since he came to have doubts about the divinity of Christ). Rather, this verse is the beautiful expression of an ideal – how Christians *ought* to feel about the sacrificial death of Jesus, and perhaps how they hope to feel one day. The same observation applies to the arias and choruses of J. S. Bach's celebrated Passions. These were written to be performed on Good Friday in the context of the biblical account of Jesus' trial, punishment, and death. They are powerful operatic expressions of grief and remorse, but these emotions are not to be attributed to Bach, his unknown librettist, the musicians who sang them, or the people who heard them. Rather, they hold up an ideal of feeling – how the mystery of Christ's death ought to affect us – and by holding up

this ideal during the liturgical observation of Good Friday they may help
to engender something of the feeling itself.

Image and Belief

The liturgical use of religious poetry for the purpose of giving expression
to ideals of devotional religious feeling is especially well illustrated by the
Jewish *Book of Psalms*, one of humanity's most enduring collections of
religious poetry. These ancient poems have the status of holy writ for both
Jews and Christians. Their origins and the dating of their collection are
obscure, but they are known to have been in liturgical use at least since
the sixth century BCE and have been continuously used in worship ever
since, up to and including the present day. These religious poems have not
only appealed to worshippers across millennia, they have also been incorporated into the worship of a large number of religious denominations
that are otherwise highly diverse in their beliefs and practices.

The psalmists, whoever they were, address God and other human
beings with sentiments of lament, fearfulness, joy, praise, longing, and
on occasions violent loathing. It is powerful evidence of the success with
which they do this, that they have been translated into many different
languages and cast into different metrical forms. At the same time, this
raises a question. If, as was suggested earlier, the aim of poetry is to give
expression to ideas and emotions in sets of words that cannot be improved
upon, and cannot be amended without significant loss, how can the value
of the psalms extend beyond the form and language in which they were
originally written? One answer, though not the most important, notes the
possibility that translations and adaptations can have a poetic value independent of the value of the originals. This can be true of any poetry. The
Irish poet and Nobel Laureate Seamus Heaney (1939–2013) translated
the Old English poem *Beowulf*. This was widely regarded as a fine poetic
achievement in its own right and won a prize for the brilliance with which
it captured the feel of Old English in modern verse. Something similar can
be said about the translations of the Psalms by Myles Coverdale (1488–
1569). Coverdale was an English Bishop and author of the first complete
translation of the Bible into English, published in 1535. The translations
of the psalms that he made were then incorporated into Cranmer's *Book
of Common Prayer*. As a result, the psalms in Coverdale's translation were
both said and sung as a component of Anglican worship over many centuries. In fact, they continue to be the preferred version in many places,
even though it is now acknowledged that as translations of the original

Hebrew, they are demonstrably imperfect. Coverdale, in other words, produced poetry that was only partly connected to the original Jewish psalms, but which proved no less of an enduring poetic accomplishment in its own right.

Coverdale's version is imperfect, but not radically removed from the Hebrew original. If it were, though, that would be a case in which poetry in one language is simply the *cause* of new poetry in another language. Normally, of course, even though translation involves moving from one language to a completely different language, there is a much closer poetic connection between the original and the translated version. Poetry is more than linguistic form. No less important is the construction and manipulation of images, and translations from one language to another can successfully preserve and transmit the original imagery. Take for instance, what is probably the best known of the psalms – Psalm 23 which begins with the affirmation "The Lord is my Shepherd." This has been translated, amended, adapted, and versified in a great many versions. What they all preserve, however, is the original imagery – the shepherd with staff and crook, green pastures beside still waters, the valley of the shadow of death, and a table spread in the sight of enemies. It is this preservation of imagery that allows us to identify these as different versions of the same original.

At the most straightforward level poetic imagery offers us unusual, captivating, and/or memorable descriptions of things in the world around us – Wordsworth's "host" of daffodils "dancing" in the breeze, for example. Imagery can do more than this, however, by enabling us to think about, and to reflect on, subject matter that, for a variety of reasons, is hard (or even impossible) to capture in theoretical explanation or empirical study. Conscious experience, for example – the warmth of the sun, the smell of coffee, falling in love – is far more easily conveyed by imagery, analogy, and metaphor than by explanation or data. So too, religious ideas, convictions, and awareness are often more readily apprehended and communicated in figurative language than in the conceptual language of, say, creeds and catechisms. Indeed, if, as has often been claimed, no one has ever seen God, and being infinite, God cannot be encompassed within categories comprehensible by finite minds, then theology will necessarily fall short of genuine knowledge. In this case, the best hope for knowledge of God must lie elsewhere – in analogy and metaphor, for instance. Both of these are poetry's stock-in-trade.

Imagery, analogy, and metaphor are not confined to poetry strictly so called. They are no less evident in novels and all forms of literary art.

Some major religious texts incorporate poetry – the Hebrew Bible and the Adi Granth, for instance, but some do not. Even the Quran, however, which is much more didactic than poetic, makes extensive use of imagery. It may even be said to have a commanding and recurrent image, namely the "Path" of righteousness. "Path" is a metaphor for the way in which faithful Muslims ought to live. Where this "path" leads, and why it is worth following is also explained in metaphor, employing one of the best known of the Quran's images – "a Parable of the Garden which the righteous are promised: in it are rivers of water incorruptible; rivers of milk of which the taste never changes; rivers of wine, a joy to those who drink; and rivers of honey pure and clear. In it there are for them all kinds of fruits; and Grace from their Lord." (Sura 47. 15) It is obviously wrong to interpret this picture literally, since the Quran expressly tells us that it is a parable. Water, wine, milk, and fruit are images, and with the help of these images the believer can grasp something of the blessedness that God promises to those who faithfully submit to his will. Muslims believe that God's revelation to Muhammad is the only way human kind can know the right "path" of submission, and the Quran (in Sura 2) expressly tells us that this revelation comes to us through parables.

Poetic writing is distinguished by its use of rhythm and rhyme, alliteration, assonance, and other such devices. Sometimes these devices simply make what the poem says more memorable or appealing. This was probably what the poet Alexander Pope (1688–1744) had in mind when he referred to "what oft was thought, but ne'er so well expressed." However, the division this line presupposes – between *what* is said and *how* it is said – does not accommodate the aspiration to poetic perfection alluded to earlier. The aim of the poet, very often at least, is to forge an inseparable unity between what is said and how it is said. It is this unity that gives poetry its communicative power. If there is no better way to say it, then *what* is said must be said in just that way. Rhythm and rhyme can have a part to play in securing this unity of content and form, because the meaning of a sentence often turns on where the emphasis falls. This is what rhythm and rhyme determine, so that following their dictates, as it were, is key to saying what it says successfully. But more often it is through imagery that poetic writing secures unity of thought and expression. The well-worn metaphors of everyday speech illustrate the point. If I say that someone is a "wet blanket" I am saying something literally false, but "poetically" true. The reason we employ the metaphor is because it very difficult to say the same thing literally. What is the *literal* equivalent of being a "wet blanket"?

The art of the poet, of course, does not lie simply in using metaphors and analogies, but in fashioning fresh images (which will often be extended metaphors) that have this same paradoxical property of conveying truth by means of literal falsehood. Through a sequence of just such images, Shakespeare imaginatively articulates a view of human life (not necessarily his own, of course) when he has Macbeth say, "Life's but a walking shadow, a poor player that struts and frets his hour upon the stage and then is heard no more; it is a tale told by an idiot, full of sound and fury, signifying nothing." (*Macbeth* Act 5, Scene 5) We can gesture to the basic idea at work in this speech, but we cannot say the same thing "literally." Applied to this case we might say that Pope's dictum has much to be said in its support. Macbeth's dark nihilism may resonate with the mood of some who watch the play. To that degree it may be said to have "oft been thought." At the same time, it is wrong to conclude from this that Shakespeare's poetic expression is therefore a decorative or memorable wrapping for an independently stateable proposition. Just what the thought is, is inextricably connected to the images with which it is expressed.

The use of imagery and figures of speech extends beyond poetry into literary prose. Images may simply delight us, but as we have seen, they can also instruct us, and are regularly used to do so in religious texts. We understand something by grasping and appreciating the image through which it is represented. In this respect, literary images can function in something like the same way that visual images do. "The Good Shepherd" is familiar as both a literary and a visual image. But the visual image (leaving film aside) is relatively static. We stand before it and contemplate it. Literary images, by contrast, can be dynamic. Time must pass as we read through poems and passages of prose, and this gives them a temporal dimension that a picture lacks. It is a dimension that the writer can then use to create a dynamic within the image.

It is not hard to find examples of this in religious writing. Charles Wesley (1707–88) is widely acknowledged to be one of the greatest Christian hymn writers. Some of the verses he wrote for Methodist congregations to sing are justly reckoned to be amongst the finest religious poetry of all time. Wesley frequently takes biblical images and re-works them for devotional purposes. He does this also with biblical events. Among the 6,000 hymns that he wrote, many regard "Wrestling Jacob" as his poetic masterpiece. It takes the story of Jacob wrestling with an angel as recorded in the *Book of Genesis* (32: 24–32), and in a sequence of verses develops it into an extended image of the dynamics of conversion. Christians who sing (or read) these words are thus not only invited to contemplate an inspiring image, but to undergo a spiritual experience imaginatively.

Events such as Jacob's encounter with the angel are usually set within a larger story, and of course storytelling is another important feature of literary art, both poetry as well as prose, and in drama. When we think of storytelling, we think primarily of entertainment, and it is true, probably, that storytelling is the oldest and most universal way in which human beings entertain their children, or agreeably pass the time together. Narrative structure, however, has much more to offer than this. It is a basic form of understanding, possibly the most basic form, since it is highly intuitive. Children understand narratives far earlier, and far more easily, than they understand inductive generalizations or theoretical explanations. Narrative's intuitive appeal, however, does not confine it to early life or simple storytelling. It is key, obviously, to biography and history. Knowing the story of someone's life, or the history of a culture, is an attested way of coming to a better understanding of people, places, and times. As these examples imply, narrative structure is not the preserve of literary art, but it does seem to have a special place there. The difference is that history and biography must root their narratives in empirical evidence, whereas literary art is free to construct narratives in accordance with the writer's imagination.

The prevalence of stories in the world's religious literature is striking, but they do not all fall into the same type. Some are clearly parables or fables. Others are no less clearly intended to be historical narratives, while others are best thought of as myths. These categories are not precise, and classifying a religious story in one of these ways can prove contentious. It is important, though, to recall the discussion of the "fictional" and the "fanciful" from the first part of this chapter. As we saw, it is wrong to think of all imaginary narratives as fanciful, since many that are not historical are nevertheless highly realistic. In any case, as the Parable of the Good Samaritan shows, the question of whether there is something to be learned from a story may not turn on its historicity at all. In common speech "myth" is often taken to imply something false and fanciful, but with respect to religious myths it may be more important to distinguish between "living" and "dead" than between "true" and the "false." Too great a concern with historical validity easily deflects us from acknowledging that myths can embody and convey significant messages – a point that applies as much to those who take myths literally as to those who dismiss myths as "fairy tales." The most important observation in the present context is that some myths have so great a power to compel the imagination, that they provide templates through which both personal and collective experience becomes meaningful.

An especially good example of this is to be found in the story of the Exodus. In the *Book of Genesis*, the story is told of a famine that drives the sons of Jacob to Egypt in search of food. There, through the good offices of their brother Joseph (whom Jacob had long believed lost, but who had become the right-hand man to Pharoah, King of Egypt), they are welcomed and generously provided for. As a result the whole Hebrew people become residents of Egypt. Following the death of Joseph, the *Book of Exodus* takes up the story. It opens with a later Pharoah, who never knew Joseph, and under whose regime the Hebrews have effectively become slaves. By chance a Hebrew baby boy, Moses, escapes this fate, and is raised as an Egyptian. Years later, though, Moses is called by God to acknowledge the Hebrews as his own people, and instructed to lead them out of their bondage to a divinely Promised Land. After God brings down a series of plagues on the Egyptians, Pharoah lets the Israelites go, and they embark on an arduous journey through a desert wilderness.

The account of their deliverance is complex and their journey to the Promised Land protracted, but the story as a whole is key to Jewish identity and religious practice. Devout Jews remember the Exodus in daily prayer, and it is celebrated each year in Pesach – the feast of Passover, a subject to be returned to. *Exodus* is also a book in the Christian Bible, of course, and provides some of the readings for the great Easter Vigil, a principal feast in the Christian calendar.

Archaeologists have failed to find anything that would lend historical support to the story of the Exodus. There is no surviving evidence that the Hebrews were ever in Egypt, or enslaved there, and no evidence of a forty-year journey through the wilderness. Scholarly consensus seems to be that, contrary to the bible story, the Israelites did not drive out the Canaanites to occupy a divinely promised land, but were, more likely, closely related to the original tribe in "the Promised Land," or even part of it themselves. It is impossible to prove a negative, so the absence of evidence cannot be taken to be conclusive, and the story of the *Exodus* may, for all that we know, have a real historical basis. But does this matter? At one level it seems that it must. How can it make sense for Jews to praise God for delivering them out of slavery if it never happened? At the same time, how could it be reasonable to expect devout Jews to suspend their religious commitment until the (impossibly distant) time at which archaeological investigations come up with a more definite answer? It seems even less reasonable to suggest that ordinary wayfaring Jews with no special expertise should undertake these investigations themselves.

But in the absence of answers to these historical questions, why *do* Jews believe in the Exodus? The answer is that, regardless of its historicity, it has proved a remarkably powerful narrative template. In his book *Exodus and Revolution*, the political philosopher Michael Walzer traces the astonishing number of historical contexts in which the narrative structure of the Exodus, together with its key concepts and images, have been called upon to illuminate and inspire political movements. Walzer's compelling study had its origins in a sermon he heard in a small Baptist church in Montgomery, Alabama, where the *Book of Exodus* was made to speak to the political struggle of southern blacks.

> There on his pulpit, the preacher, whose name I have long forgotten, acted out the "going out" from Egypt and expounded its contemporary analogues: he cringed under the lash, challenged the pharaoh, hesitated fearfully at the sea, accepted the covenant and the law at the foot of the mountain. The sermon struck me with especial force because I was, in 1960, a graduate student writing a dissertation on the Puritan Revolution [in 17th century England], and had read many sermons in which the Book of Exodus figured as a central text or a reiterated reference. Indeed, in a long speech opening the first session of the first elected parliament of his protectorship, Oliver Cromwell described the Exodus as "the only parallel of God's dealing with us that I know in the world ..."[5].

The Puritan Revolution and the American civil rights movement were both religiously inspired. They are just two of several examples that Walzer studies in some detail. Here, however, it is not the particular cases he recounts that matter, but rather the general truth they illustrate. Irrespective of their basis in history religious narratives can inform the understanding of present reality, giving it shape and meaning. More importantly, they do this with respect to living through and in the light of that experience. In other words, the understanding that the narrative offers is neither theoretical nor historical, but practical. Its principal focus is not belief but action, and as Walzer's description of the preacher he heard suggests, this leads us to another branch of literary art – drama.

Ritual and Rationality

Chapter 3 noted the tendency we have to intellectualize religion and think of it primarily in terms of theological beliefs. There are both philosophical and religious objections to this tendency, objections that point to

---

⁵ Michael Walzer, *Exodus and Revolution* (New York: Basic Books, 1985) p. 3

the importance of emotion and will. Arguably, though, there is another dimension of religion even more significant than these. Believing, feeling, and willing are things that individuals do, but individuals are very rarely religious on their own. Religion, like politics, is for the most part communal, and the vast majority of religious "believers" are to be identified as such not in terms of propositions to which they assent, but by their membership of religious communities, and their participation in the corporate actions of specific religious traditions.

The phenomenon of religious participation can be found on a scale far larger than participation in any other dimension of human life. No political rallies or rock concerts come anywhere near in size to the mass observances of, for instance, Muslims and Hindus. The largest annual gathering of human beings anywhere on earth is the Arba'een Pilgrimage held at Karbala in Iraq. In some years it has reached the astonishing number of twenty two million Shi'ite Muslims, gathered from around forty countries. This huge number even exceeds the Hajj, one of the Five Pillars of Islam, an annual pilgrimage to Mecca that adult Muslims across the world, if they are able to make the journey, are obliged to undertake at least once in their lifetime. Even vaster than either of these, though held every twelve years rather than annually, is Kumbh Mela, a mass Hindu ritual when as many as thirty million people bathe in the sacred river Ganges.

The Arba'een Pilgrimage, the Hajj, and Kumbh Mela are simply dramatically impressive instances of the kind of action that lies at the heart of religion, namely corporate ritual. Most of the time, of course, this takes place in far smaller groups and in much more modest forms. (In Judaism the *minyan* (prescribed quorum) for prayer is just ten adults). However small the number, religious rituals are nonetheless corporate. They include such things as communally recited prayers, often with coordinated bodily movements, choral and congregational singing, pilgrim journeys, rites of passage, purification and initiation, ritual sacrifice, and the dedication and consecration of places and people. As the etymologies of the words "sacrifice" and "consecration" imply, the purpose of these actions is "making holy." Indeed, this may be said to be the aim of religious ritual in general. Ritual acts lift people, places, things, occasions, and relationships out of the ordinary, and give them a significance that in some way transcends the limits and particularities of time and space.

As an anthropological description of human religion, this may be unproblematic. From a philosophical point of view, however, ritual action is puzzling. The theory of rational action we commonly apply to human conduct makes it difficult to explain how ritual action could ever be rational. By "the theory of rational action" I mean the long-standing philosophical attempt to connect reason and action in a way that both explains and justifies the universal practice of differentiating between actions properly so called, and other sorts of events, processes, and movements. Eating my dinner is an action. Digesting it is not; it is simply something that happens to the food I have consumed. Eating is rational action, digesting is causal process. Both actions and processes take place in time. So what marks out rational action from the general category of causal event?

Unfortunately, answering this question easily becomes confused because the English word "rational" has two opposites – "non-rational" and "irrational." The stomach's digestion of food is non-rational i.e. to be explained without appeal to reasons, but precisely because it is "non-rational" it cannot be "irrational." It is the distinction between the "rational" and "non-rational," not between "rational" and the "irrational" that we are concerned with here. In order for it to make sense to declare an action "irrational" (i.e. without sufficient justification), it has to be the sort of thing that *could* be rational. In this sense, "non-rational" behavior is to be contrasted with "irrational" action no less than "rational" action.

Some of the things we do, we do by instinct – stepping out of the way of danger, for example, and instinctual behavior is non-rational. It can be highly effective, nevertheless, in helping us negotiate practical matters. Instincts guide animals very successfully in their search for food, shelter, and sexual partners, and human beings (who are animals biologically speaking) also have valuable instincts. There is this important difference, however. Human beings have a faculty of reason on which they can call to anticipate needs, deliberate over possible courses of action, plan how best to spend their time, and choose between alternative strategies. Behavior guided by instinct can fail to attain its goal. When it does, this is because the instinct in question has malfunctioned in some way. Reason can recognize, accommodate, and offset this malfunction. Reason too can go wrong. When it does, the actions it motivates are irrational, though not necessarily harmful or unsuccessful. Rational choices can produce outcomes quite different to the ones that the chooser intended.

What makes an action "rational" in the sense of "rational *or* irrational"? Rational *belief* is easily connected to reality through the concepts of truth and falsehood. The precise nature of the connection is conceptually complex, but we can lay this down as a general principle of rational belief: "I ought to believe what is true, and I ought not to believe what is false." Rational *action*, however, must be different, because actions cannot be "true" or "false." Rather, they are "wise" or "foolish." While it seems right to say that a wise action is one that there are good reasons to perform, and a foolish action is one that lacks good reasons, or relies upon bad ones, this does not advance our understanding very much. It just raises another question. What makes a reason a *good* one, and how is a good reason connected to reality?

Philosophers have long drawn a contrast between instrumental and intrinsic reasons for action. Instrumental reasons confer rationality on an action by showing it to be an efficient means to a given end, and where there is a choice, the most efficient means. Conversely, irrational actions are freely chosen actions that are inefficient means to the ends in view. Thus, it is rational to undergo heart surgery if and only if this is the means to remedying the kind of heart disease I have, and more rational than preferring low doses of aspirin even if these can be expected to generate some small improvement. So I have a good reason to choose heart surgery and undergo it. Not to so choose, then, is irrational. Instrumental reasons have a connection of sorts with truths about reality, because they make the rationality of an action depend upon known generalizations about causal relations – the causes of heart disease and the effectiveness of heart surgery in this example. If the relation "A causes B" truly holds, then we have good reason to do "A" – though only if we want to bring about "B," obviously. If we don't want to do that, the fact that A *causes* B can still be true, but it does not give us any reason to act. In his *Treatise of Human Nature* (1739) David Hume argued that true generalizations about the world are the *only* connection between reason and action. Practical rationality consists in finding out facts about the world that will get us what we want, and get it more efficiently. He concluded from this that with respect to action, *reason as such* is "inert," and in a famous phrase, can only be the *slave* of the passions.

Hume's account of practical reason – that good reasons for acting are true beliefs about the most efficient means to get the things we desire – is widely shared. But since Plato, other philosophers have argued that actions can also be *intrinsically* rational. That is to say, irrespective of the ends we want to bring about, actions can be rational in and of themselves. Aquinas, for instance, holds that it is intrinsically rational to prefer a good thing to a bad one – a fresh egg to a rotten one, say. In choosing ingredients for a meal, it is certainly rational to choose them in accordance with the dish we want to eat, but it is also rational to choose them in accordance with the best available ingredients (other things being equal). On some occasions, this will give us good reason to decide on a different dish. When you go to market, if you find the chicken is fresher than the fish, choose chicken, even if you originally wanted to buy fish. Aristotle emphasizes the intrinsic value of achievement. We aim to be excellent at something – athletic prowess, say – not for the sake of any benefits it brings, but for its own sake. I *could* run a race for a purely external benefit – the impact on my blood pressure, the prize money if I win it – in which case I am acting instrumentally. But I can also want to win the race for its own sake, because I thereby show myself (to myself as well as to others) to be the fastest runner. In his *Groundwork to the Metaphysics of Morals* (1785) Immanuel Kant discusses a third possibility at considerable length, arguing that there are intrinsic reasons to perform moral actions and avoid immoral ones. Dishonest actions, Kant thinks, are *intrinsically* wrong, whether or not they get us what we want.

There is no need to resolve these philosophical differences here. We can assume that actions can be both instrumentally and intrinsically rational, because the puzzle that concerns us is this. Religious rituals do not seem to fall into either category. How, in terms of the instrumental/intrinsic distinction, should we answer the following questions? Is it rational for Christians to celebrate Holy Communion? Is it rational for Muslims to go on the Hajj? Is it rational for Jews to celebrate the Passover? If we think of these actions instrumentally, then we need to be able to say what result or consequence it is that they are efficient means to bringing about. Any specific consequence we might identify or anticipate will fall under the category of material or spiritual benefit. Religious people often do think about their rituals in this way. They suppose that prayers and incantations will protect them from danger, cure disease, or bring an end to drought and famine.

There are important objections to this way of thinking, however. If ritual actions are ways of bringing about benefits, they are rational only if they can be shown to be efficient means to those ends. How is that to be shown? Perhaps we could formulate some generalizations that are empirically tested; petitionary prayer cures cancer, for example, brings rain, or an end to war. No such generalization is likely to be plausible, however, because it is evident to everyone that even very devout people do not always get what they pray for. It is philosophically more interesting, though, to examine a background assumption to this way of thinking – that performing the ritual correctly is like using a method correctly. If we do it right, we will get the result we want.

The first point to be observed here is that construing religious ritual instrumentally turns it into a kind of magic. Magic is not conjuring.

Conjuring *appears* to be magic. It is in fact an illusion, employing ordinary causal mechanisms while cleverly hiding or disguising their use. There is no such thing as magic properly so called, but the *idea* of magic is conceptually interesting. Its ambition is to bring about effects in the world in a way that differs radically from technology. Where technology acts through the physical laws that govern the natural world, magic seeks a "short cut" in which the will and desire of human beings act *directly* on the natural world, not by manipulating it, but by telling it what to do. Traditionally, magic casts spells – special (often secret) formulae that supposedly "work" provided they are followed to the letter. These spells have no connection with known physical laws. Their aspiration, rather, is to make the natural world, including its laws, bend to the will of the magician by instructing it. The very idea of magic, then, is contrary to scientific causality, which is why in a scientific age no one really believes in magic any longer. More important in this context however, is a different conflict.

While modern secular culture tends to see magic and religion as allied, the fact is that most major religions have denounced and rejected magic as blasphemous or "impious," a religiously *improper* attitude to the spiritual world. To regard religious rituals as ways in which spiritual powers can be manipulated in accordance with human desires reduces an essentially personal relation to a purely mechanical one. In a purely mechanical relationship, however, the ideas of gift and grace have no part to play. So conceived, prayer and worship become mere techniques for getting God (or the divine) to produce spiritual "cures." A further implication of this way of thinking is that religious rituals can be dispensed with as soon as more effective medical and technological remedies come along. Consequently, ritual as magic puts a commitment to God on a purely conditional basis, to be sustained only insofar and for as long as it "works." That is why the major religions, holding the true worship of God to be unconditional, have all striven to combat magic. In short, prayers of petition and hymns are not spells or blandishments, and their true meaning is lost on anyone who thinks they are.

Contrary to what might be thought to follow from this, this argument against magic does not put paid to petitionary prayer. Just as asking other people for things can be an effective means of getting them, so asking God could be a means of getting things. But whereas medicine does not *choose* to cure diseases, God, like other agents, *chooses* how to respond to humanity's requests. Treating God as something to be manipulated for personal benefit, then, is wrong in the same way that treating other people as means instead of ends is wrong. That is where the evil of slave owning truly lies, not in the suffering and hardship that it almost invariably imposes, but in the fact that it treats a whole class of people as mere instruments to the satisfaction of the desires of a different class. It is of course conceptually impossible to enslave God. But it is no less wrong to try to do so, however absurd the attempt may be, and that is precisely what magic tries to do.

If these are good objections to construing religious rituals as means to the satisfaction of desires, and if the instrumental/intrinsic division exhausts the possibilities, then rituals must be actions performed for intrinsic reasons. At first glance this seems both a more plausible and a more attractive way of thinking. We pursue and promote excellent things because they are excellent, not because they get us what we want. On the contrary, excellence tells us what we *ought* to want. People can make money out of playing a musical instrument, and this is how many musicians earn their living. But the rationale of the musician as such is to play good music well, because that is the best thing a musician can do. If making money was the main reason, music could be abandoned without loss or regret as soon as it proved unprofitable. Intrinsic reason, in this way, seems to preserve intrinsic worth in a way that instrumentalism cannot do.

Does this rationale work for religious ritual? Do human beings engage in religious practices because they are intrinsically valuable? Before we can answer in the affirmative, there is a further question to be considered. For *whom* is the action intrinsically valuable? The answer seems obvious – for those who engage in it. But this has a curious consequence. It seems to leave out an element that is key to religious actions – worship. If the heart of religion is worshipping God (or the divine) how can its value be confined to the worshipper? It needs to be directed beyond the worshipper. But what could God, as the object of worship, get out of it?

This is one of the questions that Plato raised in the *Euthyphro*, the dialogue discussed at length in Chapter 2. In the light of that discussion, at this point a brief reminder should be sufficient. Euthyphro is on his way to prosecute his own father for an "impious" act and Socrates, with an element of irony submits him to questioning, ostensibly so that he, Socrates, may learn what true piety is. In the third part of the dialogue, Socrates draws attention to a general difficulty with the concept of religious *service*. His argument (modernized) is that since God is perfect and needs nothing that we could give, the service of God, whatever form it takes, can only benefit the worshipper and not the object of worship. But, Socrates argues, "commerce" between the human and the divine is essential to religion. That is to say, if it is to be the worship of God, it has to be a two-way relationship. Religious rituals may make us feel better. If they are not actually the service of God, then they are reduced to a form of spiritual therapy, valuable only to those who engage in it.

Some forms of religion are evidently like this. Yogic practices, and other similar exercises, can be undertaken simply for the sake of personal psychological benefit. This gives them value without reducing them to magic. Still, if this kind of practice were taken to be typical of religion as a whole, we could make little sense of much more central examples. Here we can rehearse some of the same points that were made in Chapter 2. In the Christian mass, gifts of bread and wine are presented to God at the "Offertory." If the most we can say is that this is spiritually or psychologically beneficial for those who place them on the altar, the language of "presentation" is seriously misleading. Nothing is actually being given to God. But if God can't benefit, how else could God be involved? And if God is not involved, the most we can say is that the worshipper is contemplating the divine, and no more enjoys a relationship with it than astronomers enjoy a relationship with the stars they contemplate. Besides, even if we went along with this worshipper centered way of thinking, it would have to be agreed that a religion of contemplation is too individualistic to allow us to make any sense of *corporate* ritual. Perhaps people prefer company, and so they find it more satisfactory to contemplate in one place at the same time. Still, this "convergent" contemplation no more counts as *corporate* action than fifteen people on exercise machines in the same gym would count as a "team." The conclusion seems inescapable. If, in our desire to avoid reducing religion to magic, we say that religious action is intrinsically valuable, we cannot think of it as action that reaches beyond the human and connects it with the divine.

Drama, Enactment, and Ritual

It seems then, that in order to give religious ritual a rationale – to make it intelligible – we have to set aside the instrumental/intrinsic dichotomy and find some other way of thinking about it. It is at this point that there is reason to return to the literary arts. A third rationale for action can be found in one of those arts, namely drama. This is action as "enactment."[6]

---

[6] In this context, "enactment" must be distinguished from "re-enactment." Re-enacting a historic battle, say, means faithfully following the evidence to recreate something that happened in the past. Enacting a fictional battle, on the other hand, requires creative imagination that fills out all the things on which the script is necessarily silent.

In English, the word "acting" is used widely to refer to human action in general – acting badly, acting strangely, acting as a substitute, for example – while also being used more narrowly, to mean acting on the stage or in a movie, which is to say, "playacting." Acting in this narrow sense is something that can be rationally appraised. That is to say, a part in a drama can be played well or badly, and reasons can be given for judging any given performance good or bad. What is the mark of a good performance? The player on stage can be instrumental in producing a powerful emotional response on the part of the audience. It is also true that actors and actresses can find intrinsic personal satisfaction in performing a coveted role. Yet neither of these considerations provides an adequate criterion by which acting is properly judged good or bad. A performance can both cause an unsophisticated audience to weep or laugh *and* give the performer great satisfaction, while still being a very poor one. This possibility shows that bad acting can be instrumentally and/or intrinsically valuable, and from this it follows that the mark of a good performance must lie elsewhere. Abstractly stated, we can say that the essence of acting is not to please an audience or satisfy the actor. Its principal purpose is to bring characters, actions, and interactions to life, and thus to give them manifest existence. In other words, the purpose of acting is "realization." I shall refer to this as "enacting" the people and events. The question then arises as to what exactly "enacting" involves, and how it might be relevant to religious ritual.

In the ancient Greek tragedies of Sophocles and Aeschylus the actor literally "put on" the character whose part he played by wearing a mask. This gave physical expression to an obvious distinction, the distinction between the person of the actor and the part he was playing. At the same time, it prevented the audience from confusing the two. In modern drama masks are no longer worn, but it is no less essential that the actor and the character are not conflated. It is, in fact, the mark of a poor performance if the person of the actress recognizably obtrudes into the character she plays. On the other hand, it is equally a failure if a part is simply "acted out." This is what often serves to make amateur dramatic productions unsatisfactory. The classic "ham" is not someone whose own personality displaces the character he is supposed to be playing, but someone who is *obviously* acting. Yet, if it is essential that there be no confusion between the people and the parts they play, there must nevertheless be a kind of *fusion*. Actors and actresses have to combine their own persons with that of the imagined character in such a way that the categorical distinction between the person performing and the character performed is imperceptible. In acting, something remarkable happens. A radical onto-logical gap – an actual human being *versus* an imaginary character – is bridged. One commonplace way of expressing this interesting ontological dimension in acting is to say that, for the duration of the performance, the actor must *be* the character. Katherine Hepburn, a real person, played Rose Sayer, an imaginary person, in the John Huston's film version of C. S. Forester's *The African Queen*. The fact that cinema audiences could completely identify Hepburn with Sayer is what made her performance in the role so outstanding. Precisely the same point can be made about all great performances.

The sense in which the actress can be said to *be* (and not simply *pretend to be*) the character is this. The animating spirit in a theatrical perfor-mance is the whole being of the actress – her thought, action, utterance, feeling, and physical presence. Without the person of the actress, the char-acter remains unrealized, simply a name and some lines in a script. Yet, the script remains essential; the character is not of the actress's invention, but the playwright's. Holly Golightly is a brilliantly imaginative creation in Truman Capote's novella *Breakfast at Tiffany's* (1958). In the 1961 film version, it is not through the imagination of the author, but through the acting of Audrey Hepburn (in what came to be regarded as her most successful role) that this creation is realized. The example illustrates a general truth that the imagination of the playwright or scriptwriter and the person of the actress are *both* required to make a dramatic character a reality. No amount of description or stage direction can bring the char-acter to life; only acting can do that. Furthermore, it is the role of actors, and a distinguishing mark of their art, that they realize a whole *person-ality*. They do not just perform a series of actions related to that person. This is reflected in the language that advertisements for plays and films often use, saying, "Sir Laurence Olivier *is* Richard III" and not merely "Sir Laurence Olivier *plays* Richard III."

What is special, and intriguing, about enactment, then, is that it some-how manages to combine both ontological differentiation (the actor is *not* the character) *and* ontological identification (the actor *is* the character). The skill of the actor lies in bringing this off. It is a skill because enact-ment so described can be done well or badly. This makes it rationally assessable, but not in terms of instrumental or intrinsic value. A perfor-mance is not good because it pleases the audience, or because it gives the actor the opportunity to play a famous role. As was noted before, poor performances can move and amuse audiences, and can give their performers great satisfaction, while failing to differentiate and identify the actor and the character in the right way. Great acting gives reality to inventive imagination.

What does this have to do with ritual? The answer is that many ritual observances are made most intelligible if we understand them as a form of enactment. As was argued earlier, to regard them as *instrumentally* valuable debases them by converting them into a form of magic, the attempt to bring about results in a way that circumvents the labor required by working through normal causal mechanisms. On the other hand, to regard religious rituals as *intrinsically* valuable confines their value to those who engage in them, and thereby converts them into a form of spiritual therapy. This may indeed be valued by the person who engages in it, as yoga and fitness exercises can be. Since it has no reference to anything outside itself, however, it cannot constitute a relation to the divine. The advantage to thinking of ritual as enactment is that it allows us to interpret corporate acts of religion as practices in which human agents preserve their own spatial and temporal existence, while simultaneously identifying it with something that transcends space and time.

We find this possibility realized in some of the rituals of the three great "religions of the book" – Judaism, Christianity, and Islam. The Jewish observance of Passover is a major annual festival, a remembrance commanded by the Hebrew Bible and based on some of the events related in the Book of Exodus that were considered earlier in the chapter. The central event commemorated is the liberation from slavery in Egypt under the leadership of Moses. The full festival lasts seven or eight days, but its best known ritual takes place on the first evening, the Passover Seder. This special meal, which is usually celebrated in the family home rather than the synagogue, follows a highly circumscribed, fifteen step pattern, at the heart of which the story of the Exodus is retold. Since part of the purpose of the ritual is the transmission of Jewish faith and identity from one generation to the next, the re-telling is a response to "Four Questions." It is the role of youngest child present to ask these questions, but they are not inquiries about the original story so much as about striking aspects of the ritual meal – its timing, its style, and its ingredients. The result is that while the story of God's deliverance of Israel from bondage in Egypt is retold and recalled, this is done through symbolic action, and not simply in words. The Passover Seder thus commemorates the liberation of the Israelites and their election as God's Chosen People through ritualistic enactment. Eating unleavened bread, bitter herbs, and roasted lamb, such as the ancient Jews did on the night they fled Egypt, is remembered by eating the same foods again.

The first of the four questions the child asks is: "Why is this night different from all other nights?" This question, obviously, has to be asked on the right day at the right time, i.e. the 15th day of Nisan in the Hebrew calendar (which occurs each year on a date in March or April). But in the context of this question, the expression "this night" refers *both* to the night on which the question is asked, *and* to the original Passover night. Moreover, this identification of the two times is true the next year (and every other) that the Passover is commemorated, even though, obviously, the celebration in 2016 is a different occasion from the celebration in 2017. This is further confirmation that ritual is a form of enactment. Every actor who plays Shakespeare's Richard III enacts Richard's *final* defeat at the Battle of Bosworth. And yet, this is a "finality" that has the strange property of being compatible with indefinitely many performances both before and since. Richard III *has been defeated* at the end of one performance, and yet *has not been defeated* at the start of another. David Garrick's famous performance of the scene (captured in William Hogarth's painting of 1745) and Laurence Olivier's no less famous 1955 film version of the same scene, were equally "final," despite being 210 years apart.

The central Christian ritual of the mass provides a second example of the same phenomenon. It is in fact derived from the Passover meal *via* the Last Supper, an observation of the Passover at which Jesus identifies himself with the Passover bread and wine. At the Crucifixion which follows next day, he himself then becomes the sacrificial lamb. It is this "Last Supper" that the Mass ritually enacts. In the first part of the drama, known as the "Liturgy of the Word," the "old" and "new" testaments are recounted, with readers emerging from the people just as the Hebrew and Apostolic prophets did. When the Gospel is read, however, it is carried in procession down to the people, thereby embodying the idea that the words of Jesus, unlike other prophets, are God's own. Once the Word has been heard and understood, the faithful re-affirm their faith communally, in an historic Creed.

In the second act of the drama, known as the "Liturgy of the Sacrament," ordinary bread and wine symbolizing the basic requirements of human life are placed on an altar. A prayer of consecration is said that always includes the words of Jesus at the Last Supper. The ordinary bread and wine are thus transformed into the "holy" food and drink which the faithful then consume. In this way innumerable generations of Christians are both fed by Christ, and at the same time united in "the mystical Body of Christ" with those first disciples. Here too, then, we can find the unity of singularity and repetition. Some Christian liturgies expressly declare the central action in the communion to be a commemoration of the "full, perfect, and sufficient" sacrifice of Christ on the Cross. Even so, the ritual with this action at its center may nevertheless be repeated indefinitely many times, and in indefinitely many places. Every celebration of the mass can of course be dated. It must take place in some particular location on some particular occasion. But the Mass itself is timeless, and this underlines the ritual's nature as enactment.

A central observance of Islam – the Hajj – admits of similar interpretation. Like Passover and the Mass, this pilgrimage to Mecca both looks back to Islam's past, and forms a central part of its recurrent devotional practices. The pattern of the pilgrimage was established by Muhammad, and the thousands of pilgrims who gather each year at Mecca are in part retracing the Prophet's steps, listening, for instance, to sermons from Mount Arafat on which Muhammad preached his final sermon. They are also commemorating still older events, events in the life of Abraham as recounted in the Quran. A central focus of the five-day ritual is the Kaaba, a black building within the Great Mosque of Mecca, which represents the building Abraham was commanded to construct. During the Hajj, literally millions of people circumambulate this building seven times, walking in the steps of the Prophet.

Pilgrimage to Mecca is a once in a life time obligation for able Muslims. Those who complete it record with pride the year in which they did so. In that sense it is a dateable accomplishment. But the specificity of individual observance is irrelevant. The Hajj is indefinitely repeatable and yet always remains the same. What matters is that each faithful Muslim is thereby united with every other, and with Muhammad himself.

Enactment can be done well or badly, and this is true of ritual no less than stage and screen performances. It is striking that all these examples are of highly prescribed actions. All three have guidebooks that lay down the requirements of the ritual in considerable detail. But just as no set of stage directions, however precise, can ensure a fine performance, so rituals need to be carried out with the right spirit and style. "Ritualistic" is in fact a word commonly used to capture *empty* ritual, going through the motions without the right spirit. This "spirit," however, is not an independently specifiable emotional or psychological state, any more than a ham actor can be declared a good one on the basis of his state of mind. In both cases the mind and soul of the real person must fuse with the characters and events of the drama.

The purpose of these illustrative examples is to uncover a very special connection between religion and the literary arts. Although as we saw in earlier sections of this chapter, the distinction between form and content, medium and message, is often inappropriately applied to poetry and prose, there is nonetheless a sense in which religious writing primarily *serves* the religion to which it belongs, with hymns, prayers, stories, meditations, and so on. By means of paintings, icons, and statues, the visual arts perform a similar service, and drama can do this too. The medieval mystery plays and modern nativity plays are instances of just this. But there is then this much closer relationship. Religious rituals, often, are themselves dramas.

In this chapter issues in the philosophy of the literary arts have been explored with the aim of illuminating the role of the literary arts in the practice of religion. We have seen how the concept of truth is applicable to fiction and how the devices characteristic of poetry and the literary arts more generally can be used to direct the mind to the apprehension of the kind of truths in which religion trades – truths about the realities of human existence. Rhyme, rhythm, alliteration, and figures of speech all have their part to play in this, as does creative imagery. But the literary arts also make a direct contribution to religious practice by providing a rich language for prayer, veneration, and worship, drawing very often on sacred scriptures. The use of this language for religious purposes is more often set within the context of corporate rituals. Here too, an investigation of the literary arts has some illumination to offer us, because the philosophy of drama reveals something important about the nature and intelligibility of ritualistic practices characteristic of religion.

5

Glorious and Transcendent Places

Architectural guides to the great towns and cities of the world aim to tell visitors which buildings are most worth visiting. They may highlight outstanding houses, train stations, department stores, even factories, shops, and office blocks, but by far the largest number of buildings will fall into just three categories. First, there are political buildings – palaces, parliaments, city halls, fortresses, and the like. Second, there are cultural buildings such as art museums, opera houses, and concert halls. Third, and often the largest category, are religious buildings – churches, cathedrals, monasteries, synagogues, mosques, and temples. Why is this? Such guides cannot presuppose anything about the political, cultural, or religious interests of those who use them. The guide's recommendations must rest upon aesthetic reasons. But why should it be the case that the most architecturally impressive buildings in almost any locality will include religious buildings? This chapter aims to frame an answer to this question.[1] To do so it is necessary to begin by exploring some basic issues in the philosophy of architecture.

---

[1] The title of the chapter is taken from George Herbert's poem 'The Windows' in *The Temple* (1633)

> LORD, how can man preach thy eternall word?
>   He is a brittle crazie glass:
> Yet in thy temple thou dost him afford
>   This glorious and transcendent place,
>   To be a window, through thy grace.

Architecture, Appearance, and the "Decorated Shed"

The philosophy of architecture is a relatively young subject. While architectural theory broadly construed has a long history, it was some 200 years before architecture was fully incorporated into the subject matter of the philosophical aesthetics that arose in the course of the eighteenth century. Part of the reason for this is that architecture makes little appearance in the writings of the major philosophers who laid the foundations of philosophical aesthetics. Francis Hutcheson's *Treatise* on the idea of beauty (1725) devotes just a few paragraphs to the subject, David Hume's essay *Of the Standard of Taste* (1741) makes no mention of it, and Immanuel Kant's hugely influential *Critique of Judgment* (1790) has only a few sentences here and there. Hegel's *Lectures on the Fine Art*, published posthumously in 1835, gave architecture sustained attention, but the *Lectures* were far less influential than Hegel's principal writings, and in any case, the general direction of philosophical aesthetics had already been set by then.

In the twentieth century, however, architecture, alongside music and theater, became a subject of interest to philosophical aesthetics in its own right. Philosophers moved on from their traditional focus on the abstract concepts of art, taste, and beauty to begin identifying and exploring the conceptual issues peculiar to specific art forms. In the case of architecture, two questions have subsequently emerged as being critical to their discussions. First, "Is architecture an art?" Second: "How is architecture to be distinguished from the construction of buildings in general?" This second question has regularly been articulated in a more specific form by the use of a comparison with which the architectural historian Nikolaus Pevsner opens his *Outline of European Architecture* (1943). Pevsner contrasts Lincoln Cathedral and a bicycle shed. Both are constructions, but the first very evidently is a great work of "architecture," while the second is a mere "building." These central questions at the heart of the philosophy of architecture are interconnected. If we are able to answer the first and decide whether architecture is indeed one of the arts, this generates an answer to the second. Answering the first question will determine what it is that takes construction out of the category of "mere" building, and re-classifies it as *architecture*.

It would be a mistake, though, to think of including architecture among the arts as simply a matter of empirical classification. There is an indispensable evaluative component. To declare architecture an art is to claim a special status for buildings that instantiate it. Refusing to think of architecture in this way denies such a status to *any* building. Intuitively, granting architecture the status of "art" seems to require that the value of any building so classified must in some way exceed or transcend utility and functionality. Once granted the status of "art," a work of architecture stands alongside the great works of music, painting, and literature, to be heralded as an equally significant cultural accomplishment. By implication, those who design and construct buildings that warrant this classification become more than structural engineers and join the ranks of composers, painters, novelists, and poets. Is it right to think of them in this way? That is why the question of architecture's artistic status matters.

Why should there be any problem about classifying architecture as an art? Why should anyone wonder whether architecture warrants this classification? The issue arises because with respect to architecture, functionality is indispensable. The utility of a building never ceases to be relevant. This does not seem to be true of the other arts. Indeed, the opposite is frequently thought to be the case. Other kinds of artwork need not be functionally useful at all. It is true that painting, poetry, and music do often have everyday uses, in commercial advertisements for example. Yet, what marks them off as "arts," a familiar way of thinking supposes, is their ability to dispense with all *extraneous* purpose, and still possess an autonomous, intrinsic value quite independent of the purpose they may once have served. Take, for example, the posters that Henri de Toulouse-Lautrec (1864–1901) produced for the opening of the Moulin Rouge, the famous nineteenth century musical theater in the Montmartre district of Paris. Toulouse-Lautrec's posters had a commercial purpose – to bring paying customers to the extravagant entertainments that were staged there. They have long out-lived that purpose, and the events and performers they advertised are forgotten. The posters themselves, however, continue to attract interest and admiration. That is because, regardless of their original purpose and how well or badly they served it, they have a quality that marks them out as valuable works of art in their own right.

In this respect, buildings seem quite different. There is an important sense in which they *cannot* be successfully separated from their usefulness. A building that retains its form but outlives its function – whether original or adapted – is a *redundant* building. Redundant buildings eventually decline into ruins or are demolished, thereby demonstrating how usefulness is intrinsic to them. Of course, they need not do so. Someone may decide to preserve them, keeping them structurally sound and maintaining their appearance. But preservation, as opposed to adaptation, does not find a genuine alternative use for a building. It turns it into a museum piece, something that may well be beautiful to look at, but has strictly historic interest – how people used to live, or work, or worship. Truly living buildings need to go on being useful. Yet this very fact raises a question about architecture as an art. If a building's continuing to be useful is essential, where does its *autonomous* value as an artwork lie? Where could it lie?

These questions reflect an ideal that was discussed at some length in Chapter 1 – the autonomy of art. The familiar slogan "art for art's sake" expresses this ideal. It places the essential value of a work of art wholly within that work itself. This is sometimes explained in terms of the work's "organic unity," an integration of form and content that is admirable and valuable in and for itself. With this ideal in mind, it seems that if works of architecture are to be works of art, they too must have organic unity. The problem is that their essential functionality appears to stand in the way of any such unity. That is because a building's sound construction and attractive appearance can both survive the redundancy of its purpose.

Not everyone holds that the concept of organic unity is essential to art, though it is an idea that has dominated a great deal of philosophical debate. But if there is some truth in it, then as the last sentence of the previous paragraph implies, the problem with respect to architecture appears to be even more intractable than simply the indispensability of extraneous function. The task is made more complex by the fact that in architecture there are *three* dimensions needing to be forged into a unity. The three-dimensional nature of architecture is acknowledged in writings that go back to ancient times. One of the most prestigious figures in the history of building, Marcus Vitruvius Pollio (c. 80–15 BCE), commonly known as Vitruvius, was a civil and military engineer and author of one of the earliest dissertations on architecture – *De Architectura* (now known as *The Ten Books on Architecture*). Vitruvius's work is a compendium of information rather than a systematic treatment of the subject, but it expressly identifies three factors that builders must take into consideration – appearance, function, and construction – how a building looks, what use it is meant to serve, and how it has been engineered.

Vitruvius's is an ancient voice expressing a common consensus. Architecture has usually been thought of as the achievement of excellence in all three dimensions – "commodity, firmness and delight" is another traditional way of listing these. However, the necessary co-presence of *three* distinct dimensions makes the task of conceiving their organic integration into a unified whole even more difficult, since it is easy to specify each one of the three dimensions quite independently of the other two.

That is to say, the appearance, construction, and function of a building all draw on distinct forms of activity. This suggests that their excellence needs to be judged by different criteria, just as the speed, economy, and comfort of a car are to be judged by different criteria. Whether or not a building is well constructed, for instance, is a matter of its ability to withstand stresses of various kinds and thus a matter for engineers to assess. How effectively it serves the function for which it is intended seems to be a practical judgment to be made chiefly by those who use it. The success or failure, excellence or mediocrity, of construction and function can be assessed quite independently of the building's appearance. Is appearance alone, then, the dimension that is left for "art" and the exercise of aesthetic judgment?

Suppose that we relinquish the ideal of organic unity, and declare that architecture strictly so called is only concerned with appearance. It is hard to avoid some very unwelcome implications. First, returning to Pevsner's comparison, if the only architecturally significant difference between Lincoln Cathedral and a bicycle shed is appearance, then this magnificent building is just a highly "decorated shed," to use an expression made famous by the architect Robert Venturi.[2] Secondly, distinguished in this way from the engineer, the architect is not really a builder at all, but rather simply a decorator of the surfaces on constructions that other people have built. Thirdly, in lacking any essential connection to construction, architecture becomes another exercise in visual art, conceptually indistinguishable from sculpture, even if architectural artworks are generally quite large, and accordingly "walk through" sculptures.

These simple observations are sufficient to sustain the thought that real difficulties result from abandoning the artistic ideal of organic unity and attempting to focus exclusively on appearance as the only artistically significant dimension of architecture. It is plausible to construe these difficulties as a *reductio ad absurdum*, a logical refutation of the contention that the art of architecture resides in how buildings appear. Not everyone has drawn this conclusion. John Ruskin (1819–1900), for example, the first Slade Professor of Fine Art at the University of Oxford and author of *The Seven Lamps of Architecture* (1849) was willing to bite this particular bullet. He held that the role of the architect is to imbue buildings with moral qualities, and he was willing to endorse the view that architecture does this essentially through the decoration of construction. This may indeed

---

[2] Robert Venturi, Denise Scott Brown, and Steven Izenour, *Learning from Las Vegas* (Cambridge Mass: MIT Press, 1972)

make it a visual art, but it is nevertheless distinguishable from painting pictures and sculpting figures. Or so Ruskin contended. Relatively few architectural theorists have followed him on this point, however, chiefly because architectural aestheticism of this kind too easily accommodates "façade," and the use of façade is a practice that many, possibly most architects have regarded with suspicion.

Their anxiety may be expressed in this question. If the architect's only concern is with appearances, what is to constrain, or even qualify, the deliberate creation of misleading appearances? This is precisely what façade can so easily be used to do, and often has been. Given a "classical" façade, a bank, say, assumes the character of a socially venerable building, and thus an institution with the stability and respectability that its "magnificent" appearance implies. Social venerability is not among Ruskin's seven "moral" qualities,[3] but it works in the same way. And the point is that architectural grandeur can convey, and may be meant to convey, a character quite at odds with the bank's history, its true worth or its current financial security. Similarly, to give a restaurant or hotel the appearance of a castle or a palace implies an elevated reputation that may contradict the quality of the service and accommodation that it actually offers. Façade also can mislead us about structure. The impression of structural solidity that Doric or Corinthian columns usually give, can by that very fact seriously mislead us about the permanence of the building that they have been used to face.

In short, with the clever use of façade, a building's appearance can belie, and be made to belie, its real character with respect to both function and construction. That is why both practicing architects and architectural critics have often regarded the use of façade as involving a lack of professional integrity, and held the creation of transparently "truthful" appearances to be preferable by far. But what could the "truthful" appearance of a building be truthful *to*, except to the other dimensions of architecture – construction and function?

Sometimes, this anxiety about façade seems a little precious, and it is undoubtedly the case that talk of "truthful" building can be aesthetically pretentious. Still, if we abandon the integrity of construction and appearance as an ideal, the connection between the two becomes wholly fortuitous. If architects really are decorators, albeit of unusually large constructions, why do they need to know *anything* about engineering? And why do they engage in making *buildings* at all? If their art does reside

[3] Ruskin's seven "lamps" are sacrifice, truth, power, beauty, life, memory, and obedience.

in the aesthetics of appearance, semblance *without* construction should in principle be no less of an accomplishment. Thus, from this narrowly aesthetic point of view, the houses depicted in a stage set, or the urban backdrop to a movie, though they are not actually buildings, could nevertheless display the "form" and hence the appearance of buildings. We might put the point this way. Visual *tromp l'oeil* in painted backdrop would be just as aesthetically effective as constructed *forced perspective* in an actual building, and the former would have the advantage of substantially lower costs and less effort. Locating the art of architecture in the appearance of buildings, accordingly, brings us by a different route to the same absurd conclusion – that architects can be artists without building anything. We can generalize from this conclusion. Any conception of architecture that makes the *appearance* of a building critical, is not a conception of *architecture* at all.

Architecture and "Aesthetic Ideas"

Does this unacceptable conclusion follow from abandoning the concept of organic unity, or is it a result of placing too much emphasis on the dimension of appearance? Might such an unwelcome conclusion be avoided if, while still acknowledging the importance of appearance, we were to place the main emphasis on construction instead? That is to say, would it be more satisfactory to think in terms of "the art of *building*," and seek the distinctively aesthetic element there? Arguably, just such shift of emphasis explains the displacement of the classic Palladian and Gothic styles that were so popular with architects and their clients in the nineteenth century by the "modern" architecture of the early twentieth century. A leading figure in this movement was the Swiss-French architect Charles-Édouard Jeanneret-Gris (1887–1965), much better known as Le Corbusier. Le Corbusier's architectural manifesto of 1931 was significantly entitled *Towards a New Architecture*. In it, he distanced his thinking from the much more aesthetic focus of Ruskin and others in the nineteenth century, emphatically declaring that architecture has nothing to do with the various "styles." "The styles of Louis XIV, XV, XVI, or Gothic, are to architecture what a feather is on a woman's head; it is sometimes pretty, though not always, and never anything more."[4] "Prettiness", in other words, is not what architecture is about. Indeed,

---

[4] Le Corbusier, *Towards a New Architecture* 13th edition, trans. Frederick Etchells (New York: Dover Publications, 1986) p. 37

the main point of Le Corbusier's book is to issue "three reminders to architects," and these "reminders" point away from aesthetic appearance to "mass," "surface," and "plan" as the dimensions of architecture that really matter. Architecture, Le Corbusier says in a much quoted phrase, is the "masterly, correct and magnificent play of masses, brought together in light." "Our eyes," he continues, "are made to see forms in light; light and shade reveal these forms; cubes, cones, spheres, cylinders or pyramids are the great primary forms which light reveals to advantage."[5]

This reference to "our eyes" might be taken to suggest that, despite his determination to abandon considerations of "style," Le Corbusier has actually failed to escape the emphasis on appearance as architecture's principal concern. To a degree, this is correct. The play of masses brought together in light is evidently something we are invited to contemplate with admiration. Contemplation, however, is not confined to the visual. The principal reference, after all, is to *three-dimensional* shapes, and the "cubes, cones, spheres and cylinders and pyramids" by which the architect has formed the space that the building both creates and occupies can only be properly appreciated by walking through and past them. That is what differentiates an actual building from stage flats or backdrops that offer the appearance of "buildings." However attractive and impressive an appearance they may present, they are two-dimensional.

Le Corbusier's book is not a philosophy of architecture, or even a systematic architectural treatise. But it does contain a promising idea; it is in the construction of spaces that we will find the key to architecture as a distinctive and autonomous art. All building creates a shaped space, but in architecture properly so called, Le Corbusier suggests, the cubes, cylinders, and so on, are forged into a unified whole by a "plan" that relates them to each other. Architecture, he writes, is

a profound projection of harmony [and] the plan is at its basis...Without plan there can be neither grandeur of aim and expression, nor rhythm, nor mass, nor coherence. Without plan we have the sensation...of shapelessness, of poverty, of disorder, or wilfulness.[6]

This appeal to "the plan" is what enables Le Corbusier to distinguish architecture from decoration. Its role, he says explicitly, is to make diversity "the result of *architectural principle* and not of *the play of decoration.*"[7]

[5] Ibid.   [6] Ibid., p. 51   [7] Ibid., emphasis added

But what exactly is a "plan" in this sense? Does it secure the essential aesthetic component that would make architecture an art? And if so, how? Le Corbusier's text is not very informative when it comes to answering these questions, but we can find some illumination if we place his general thought in the broader context of the Kantian aesthetic recounted at some length in Chapter 1. Kant himself, as was noted earlier, does not have very much to say about architecture. At the same time, his profound influence in philosophical aesthetics also extended to architectural thinking, and even to the practice of architecture. The historian of aesthetics Paul Guyer, has observed that "Kant's thesis that all art involves the expression of 'aesthetic ideas,' brought about a shift in architectural thinking from an essentially Vitruvian conception of architecture, according to which its two chief goals are beauty and utility, to a cognitivist or expressivist conception of architecture, in which, like other forms of fine art, architecture is thought of as expressing and communicating abstract ideas."[8] Could Le Corbusier's "plan" be construed as a Kantian "aesthetic idea"? To answer that question, obviously, we must first explain what an "aesthetic idea" is.

Kant devotes a number of sections of the *Critique of Judgment* to the topic. The following is a key passage.

> The aesthetic idea is a representation of the imagination, associated with a given concept, which is combined with such a manifold of partial representations in the free use of the imagination that no expression designating a determinate concept can be found for it, which therefore allows the addition to a concept of much that is unnameable, the feeling of which animates the cognitive faculties and combines spirit with the mere letter of language.[9]

Like so much of the *Critique*, this passage is very difficult to understand. For present purposes, however, it is enough to grasp the general thrust of Kant's contention. This is the thought that beautiful art (or a lot of it) has quasi-*cognitive* as well as *sensuous* content. It cannot be appreciated by the senses alone; there is also something to be understood. When we contemplate a great work of art we do not merely delight in its appearance – color, shape, tone, organization, and so on. We also relish the profusion of thoughts and imaginings that it stimulates within us. Kant finds aesthetic ideas at their most evident in the art of poetry.

[8] Paul Guyer, 'Kant and the Philosophy of Architecture', *Journal of Aesthetics and Art Criticism* 69 (1) (2011) p. 7
[9] Kant, *Critique of Judgment* §49

The poet ventures to make sensible rational ideas of invisible beings, the kingdom of the blessed, the kingdom of hell, eternity, creation, etc., as well as to make that of which there are examples in experience, e.g. death, envy, and all sorts of vices, as well as love, fame etc., sensible beyond the limits of experience, with a completeness that goes beyond anything of which there is an example in nature.[10]

This concept of "aesthetic idea" is helpful in explicating an important dimension of artistic and aesthetic assessment that a simple reliance on beauty cannot accommodate. Within the category of the beautiful, it seems, we can distinguish between the more and less profound. A simple folk tune and a major symphony can both be beautiful, as can a short story and a novel on the scale of Tolstoy's *War and Peace*. To rank "profound" art works about merely "attractive" works, we need to find some criterion other than beauty. At the same time, this second criterion must not remove an artwork from the realms of the aesthetic, as it would be removed if we focused on its value as historical evidence, or its recreational benefits, or even its potential to be morally edifying. All these would be reasons to value more complex and sophisticated works of art over simpler ones, but they would not be the right kind of reason. By contrast, Kant's conception of the different degree to which works of art make things "sensible [i.e. able to be apprehended] beyond the limits of experience" is the right kind of reason (though Kant gives no indication that he would use it in this way). The important point, however, is this. If it is true that beautiful works of art can give sensuous expression to things that are *beyond* the limits of sense experience, then they must have something beyond *aesthetic form*, which is limited to sensuous appearance, and embody *aesthetic ideas*.

But how could works of art make things "sensible beyond the limits of experience"? It seems a contradiction in terms. If an artwork is accessible to the sense of sight or sound, how could it at the same time go *beyond* the limits of experience? Fortunately, Kant has given us a few suggestions about what he has in mind – invisible beings, heaven, hell, eternity, the creation of the world, death, envy, love, fame. All of these are things that we cannot experience directly through the senses. Nevertheless, things that we *can* experience through the senses – visual images, musical sounds, rhymes, and rhythms – have the power, somewhat strangely, to convey what lies beyond them. There are many religious paintings of angels and of heaven, and poems about hell (Dante's *Inferno*, most famously). Love and envy can be apprehended, though they cannot be seen, in poetry and

---

[10] Ibid.

dramatic works. These are good examples of what Kant has in mind, and they illustrate his point. We will all die, yet death is not an *experience* we will undergo. So death *itself* is "beyond the limits of experience." Nevertheless, a powerful depiction of "the Grim Reaper," for instance, can visually prompt a "profusion of thoughts" about death. It is thus an "aesthetic idea."

How does the notion of "aesthetic idea" apply to architecture? As was noted in Chapter 1, a proposition that underlies the Kantian aesthetic is that art has purposefulness, but is without purpose. Le Corbusier's concept of a "plan" might be said to lend a building purposefulness in just this sense; it uses geometrical figures to shape space meaningfully by constructing a building that can be walked in and around purposefully. Purposeful occupancy of this kind is elevated to an experience of art insofar as we can say that it allows us to apprehend "rational ideas of invisible beings" as well as aspects of the human condition, such as death, eternity, or perfection, that go "beyond the limits of experience."

On the face of it, this line of thought is very promising for the philosophy of religious architecture. Why are major works of architecture so often churches, temples, and mosques? It is not hard to see how Le Corbusier's emphasis on construction over "style" or appearance combined with Kant's conception of aesthetic ideas as the foundation of great art, might be made to generate an answer. The artistic importance and social prominence of religious architecture, it suggests, can be explained in terms of the "aesthetic ideas" that these impressive buildings present to the senses of those who view them. Experiencing the structured spaces of great Gothic cathedrals, Romanesque abbeys, Orthodox churches, Hindu temples, Buddhist shrines, and so on, stimulates our imagination to the sensuous apprehension of religious ideas that go beyond the limits of experience in just the way that Kant suggests – God, redemption, mortality, eternity, heaven, and the like. That is to say, the architectural "plans" of these magnificent buildings sensuously embody ideas that are properly described as "transcendent." They facilitate the apprehension of mortality by intimations of immortality, so to speak, and gesture toward a divine perfection that casts a quite different perspective on human achievements. It is further confirmation of this suggestion that people have regularly been inclined to speak about the architectural features of religious buildings in precisely this way. Without any special prompting they see large domes as analogues of the canopy of the heavens over the earth, delicate spires as pointers to a transcendent God, vast sets of steps as physical embodiment of a spiritual "Jacob's ladder"', and so on. These

are all shapes and masses that architects can use to set religious buildings apart from everyday life, thereby prompting ideas that go beyond
human experience in a way that also marks its limits. The infinite, in
other words, is revealed, albeit imperfectly, by a sensuous presentation
of the finite.

There are a number of advantages that this way of thinking has over the
focus on appearance considered in the previous section. First, it preserves
the distinctive character of architecture as building. Second, it enables
us to explain how buildings can rightly be included in the category of
great works of art alongside paintings, poems, and musical compositions.
Third, it accommodates purposefulness in a fashion that is consistent with
the widely accepted Kantian account of aesthetic value and artistic autonomy. It thus lends functioning buildings a value greater than simple utility.
Fourth, it offers us an account of what is special about religious buildings,
namely that they embody distinctively religious "aesthetic ideas." These
are all considerable advances. Yet there is one important consideration
that weighs against it, namely that Kant himself qualifies the application
of his account of art and aesthetics to architecture. In another section of
the *Critique* he takes up the question.

[T] he beauty ...of a building (such as a church, a palace, an arsenal, or a garden
house) presuppose[s] a concept of the end that determines what the things should
be, hence a concept of its perfection, and is thus merely adherent beauty ...[T]he
combination of the good (that is, the way in which the manifold is good for the
thing itself, in accordance with its end) with beauty does damage its purity. One
would be able to add much to a building that would be pleasing in the intuition
of it, if only it were not supposed to be a church.[11]

Once again, this is not a very easy passage to understand. When Kant
speaks of "adherent" beauty, he is referring to beauty in some sense "additional to" a beautiful object rather than an integral part of it. Applied
to the present case his thought is this. A functioning building such as a
church or palace can be said to have aesthetic value because those who see
it are prompted to have a profusion of thoughts as well as sensations. It
is this profusion of thoughts that gives the building aesthetic purposefulness, a purposefulness that the imagination can apprehend and appreciate.
However, a functioning building also has a specific *purpose*, and purposefulness *without purpose* is preferable for the sensual presentation of an
aesthetic idea. That is because, Kant seems to think, utilitarian interests
damage the "purity" of aesthetic appreciation. Aesthetic appreciation is

---

an essentially "disinterested" attitude, and is therefore in tension with a practical attitude, since asking whether a building serves its purpose well or not is asking an "interested" question.

In the case of churches, Kant's point might be made persuasively by adapting the final sentence of the passage quoted. "There is much added to a church building that is pleasing in the intuition of it *once it has become a ruin.*" Ruined churches have lost their purposes, but not their *purposefulness.* That is why they do not cease to stimulate the imagination to transcendental ideas when they fall into ruin. On the contrary, ruins like Solomon's temple or the Abbey at Rievaulx are often valued and cited as *heightening* a sense of the holy, transience, mortality, heaven, and the like. If that is true, it seems to support Kant's contention that the aesthetic ideas expressed in buildings are *more* apparent when they cease to be in use. That is because no one is any longer deflected by a concern about their usefulness.

In this respect, it is worth noting, religious buildings may differ from ruined "arsenals" or "garden houses" (to use Kant's own examples). A fortress that falls completely out of use can continue to be of aesthetic interest as a space set apart by shape and mass. But it will not retain anything of the "ideas" of safety and security that might be said to be its "plan." Similarly, a ruined house, whatever its beauty, no longer embodies the aesthetic idea of a home. In both cases the ruin effectively becomes a walk-through statue. This can of course be the case with ruined churches and abbeys, many of which retain too few of their original architectural features to prompt a "profusion" of anything. But it does seem to be the case that people often experience religious "aesthetic ideas" when they contemplate the ruins of churches and temples.

We must conclude, then, that though explaining the special architectural status of churches in terms of the distinctively religious aesthetic ideas that they prompt is initially very promising, in the end it proves inadequate. Unlike ruins, *functioning* churches and temples cannot merely have purposefulness; they necessarily have to serve a purpose, and to do it well. If, as Kant alleges, this detracts from their capacity for "free" as opposed to "attendant" beauty, then his account of aesthetic ideas cannot be fruitfully combined with Le Corbusier's concept of a spatial plan.

A closely related point has in fact been made about Le Corbusier's own architectural construction. In his attempt to move away from traditional styles and methods of house building, he developed the concept of the *machine à habiter,* a "machine for living." This was the basis of a whole series of buildings, the first and most famous being the *Cité radieuse*

(Radiant City) in Marseilles, France. Built between 1947 and 1952, and better known now by its generic name – *Unité d'habitation* – the design proved enormously influential among urban planners, and is often cited as the inspiration of the modernist apartment blocks that subsequently became a feature of cities across Europe and America. Notoriously these blocks proved to be most unsatisfactory as places in which to live, and a great many were subsequently demolished. Arguably, this is a result of the fact that Le Corbusier's principal focus was on architectural "shapes and masses." As one commentator has remarked, "it is when the machine is *contemplated* that it is found to be architecture, not when it is being *used*." [12] And whatever their merits when simply contemplated, machines for living proved intolerable when they were used.

Architecture and the Aesthetics of Everyday Life

The Vitruvian conception makes beauty and utility the twin goals of architecture, but it characterizes the activity as a whole in terms of three dimensions – appearance, construction, and function. The philosophical question is how these three dimensions can be integrated to form the sort of unity that could make a building a work of art. We have explored two prominent lines of thought, both of which attempt to secure this unity by placing the main emphasis on one of these dimensions in relation to the other two. The first takes the appearance of a building to be its principal aesthetic dimension. However plausible this may seem initially, it has the odd and unacceptable consequence of reducing architecture to decoration, a visual art that need not be connected with building at all. In response to this deficiency, theorists like Le Corbusier made construction the main emphasis. Again this is plausible because architecture clearly does involve the planned creation of three-dimensional spaces. Their being planned opens up the possibility of an interesting connection with Kant's conception of "aesthetic ideas," and this is especially promising when we are thinking about the architecture of religious buildings. It enables us to explain how the most impressive of these buildings are not simply very beautiful, but convey and resonate with transcendent ideas that mark them out as religious. Still, further reflection shows that the "aesthetic ideas" that the appearance and construction of such buildings can undoubtedly prompt, does not require them to be functioning

[12] Andrew Ballantyne, 'Architecture, Life and Habit', *Journal of Aesthetics and Art Criticism* 69 (1) (2011) p. 46, emphasis added

churches or temples. Indeed, sometimes it seems, ruins are more effective in this respect.

A third possibility clearly waits to be examined. Could we find artistic unity in works of architecture by concentrating on function as the primary focus? The suggestion that we can gives rise to what may be called a "pragmatist aesthetic." This way of thinking starts with the supposition that aesthetic appreciation must arise from the experience of *using* a building, not simply admiring its appearance, or disinterestedly contemplating its spatial form. A pragmatist aesthetic, in other words, connects *building* well with *living* well. A good house is one that is good to live in, but "goodness" here cannot be confined to strictly utilitarian properties like convenience and economy. It also includes aesthetic properties like elegance and charm, and structural properties like being wind and water tight. The fact that a house is ugly, is a good reason not to want to live in it, even if it is soundly built and inexpensive to run. In a similar fashion, a courtroom that serves its function well is not only one in which it is easy to speak and to be heard, but one that "looks the part," i.e. has a grandeur and solemnity appropriate to the seriousness that surrounds the administration of justice. In the same way, to say that a church is good to worship in is a matter not just of sightlines and acoustics, but appearance and "feel." Some churches successfully convey prayerfulness, others do not.

As a way of thinking about building and architecture, this alternative pragmatic aesthetic has a number of valuable features. First, it succeeds in unifying function, construction, and appearance rather neatly, as the examples just given attest. All three are indispensable to the assessment of the quality of a building. Second, this unity is grounded in the assessment and appreciation of buildings within the general context of practical activity. This is a major shift away from the aesthetics of the eighteenth century. It removes any necessity for architecture to stake its claim to a rightful place among the "fine" arts, and instead locates architectural aesthetics within what has come to be known as "the aesthetics of everyday life," a topic that was introduced in the course of Chapter 1. As we saw in that chapter, the aesthetics of "art for art's sake" transformed the eighteenth century distinction between "the fine arts" and "the mechanical arts." It elevated the former to "Art" or "art proper" and reduced the latter to "craft" or "Design." This new distinction came to dominate philosophical thought about art and beauty in general. The resulting division between Art and Design not only shaped the activities of the art world, but also separated the "high" art of the museum, the gallery, the theater, the lecture room, and the concert hall from the activities of everyday life. Yet, though these developments in thinking about art and aesthetics had great cultural influence and widespread consequences, beauty and artistry never ceased to matter far beyond the confines of the art world. The worlds of Design – fashion, furniture, cookery, décor, folk music, gardening, recreation, and so on – did not relinquish their interest in aesthetic quality, and leave everything to "Art." There continued to be an aesthetics of the *everyday*, not confined to special times or designated places, but pervading the daily life of human beings in almost every aspect.

The world of the everyday is a pragmatic one, concerned with earning a living, getting things done, making a home, raising a family, teaching, and learning. In all these things, aesthetic judgment matters just as much as it does in concert halls, museums, grounds for sculpture, or literary competitions. People want to dress beautifully, to decorate their homes and furnish them elegantly, to serve good food on fine china, to drink excellent wine from beautiful glassware, to teach their children to use their natural language to good rhetorical effect. They want to own cars that are as satisfying to look at as they are to drive. Pragmatist aesthetics lays great store by these facts. Sometimes an emphasis on the aesthetics of the everyday is taken to imply that "high" art – the art of the museum, the gallery, the concert hall, and so on – is nothing more than a cultural imposition, the social elevation of the aesthetic tastes and preferences of the upper classes over others. No doubt there is often some truth in this, but a pragmatist aesthetic does not have to carry any such implication. No one need deny that the music of Beethoven, for instance, is an artistic accomplishment that far exceeds even the most beautiful and attractive of folk music, or that this makes Beethoven's musical genius quite exceptional. Similarly, everyone can happily concede that there is an important aesthetic gap between the paintings of Jackson Pollock and even the most expensive wallpaper. On the other hand, it is no less groundless for the enthusiast of the art of the museum and the concert hall to suppose that everyday life is an *inferior* context for the exercise of aesthetic judgment. Good "taste" is as important in choosing a restaurant in which to eat as it is in choosing which recital or play to attend.

A pragmatist aesthetic has a third important feature. It makes "fittingness" an important aesthetic consideration. This is because, by making aesthetic judgment part of daily living, it necessarily locates all such judgments in that context. The autonomy of "art for art's sake," by contrast, constructs its own special context. Music, for example, is offered to audiences in acoustically suitable concert halls, protected from the competing sounds of the street, the household, and the market place. Or else it is listened to through headphones, a practice which has the same effect. Paintings and sculptures are displayed in purpose built (or adapted) art museums, to be viewed in galleries where the lighting and the décor are designed to serve the contemplation of the art works. Drama is given the exclusive use of a stage that has no purpose other than theatrical productions. This privileged context sets high art apart from the art of the everyday. Fashion, furniture, cookery, décor, folk music, gardening must display their aesthetic qualities in competition with the world around them. This means that they have to be fitting for, and to, their context as that context happens to be. It is possible, for instance, to be elegantly dressed for one occasion when appearing in precisely the same outfit on another occasion would be "overdressed." Wallpaper that would truly grace a large room becomes too grand when it is used to cover the walls of a small one. Rhythms and images that would make a verbal tribute beautifully suited to one occasion could make it impossibly pompous and "arty" on another.

The criterion of "fittingness" to context has direct application to architecture. Functioning buildings cannot be isolated from their site and environment either by intent or in effect. A building always has a location, a context that in part determines its aesthetic success. A building that would be magnificent in one location could be absurdly out of place in another, towering over the others that surround it, or dwarfed by them and made to look ridiculously small. A building that would make a good impression set high on a hill, might fail to make any impression on level ground. The point applies not just to buildings *as a whole*, but to the architectural "vocabulary" that the architect chooses to incorporate in their design. Columns that lend a real sense of grandeur to a building in one location may degenerate into the unattractively grandiose in another. Odd though it sounds, it is possible for a building to be grotesquely grand. Castellation on a cottage, for example, very rarely "works."

In the eighteenth century, landscape gardeners in Britain and France often erected little Roman temples, Chinese pagodas, Egyptian pyramids, ruined abbeys, or Tatar tents in the parks and gardens of palaces and stately homes. These were there to add aesthetic interest, to surprise, to be admired and enjoyed, when people took their recreational walks. They were called "follies." This is an architectural term applied to small buildings that have no practical purpose, or whose purpose (storing horticultural equipment perhaps) is dramatically less important than their extravagant design would suggest. Follies may be said to be architecture as an "art," because they are identifiable "artworks" comparable to painting and poetry. Since such buildings are effectively divorced from function, however, they are exceptional. They cannot be the norm. What this shows is that if *serious* architecture is to be an art, it must find and display its credentials in the aesthetics of everyday life. It is this fact that makes a pragmatist aesthetic seem the most promising for architecture.

Architecture and Social Significance

"Fittingness" to the places and purposes of everyday life, then, is a key concept in the aesthetics of architecture, and it applies to modest buildings no less than grand ones. This explains the fact that factories, gate lodges, shops, and train stations can appear in architectural guidebooks alongside the sorts of buildings that interest Kant – "a church, a palace, an arsenal, or a garden house." However, precisely because this is so, we are left with the question with which we began. Why is it that *some* kinds of building dominate such guidebooks? In particular, why are churches, temples, and mosques special?

The first remark to make is that not all are. It is notable that some religious groups have resisted any inclination to make their places of worship architecturally impressive. The Society of Friends (or Quakers) for instance, built meeting houses rather than churches and deliberately kept them simple. Some are to be found in architectural guidebooks, but only for the same sort of reasons that a gatehouse or shop might be. Similarly, the mosques of Wahhabi Muslims generally do not have minarets, for fear of succumbing to unworthy ostentation. Even mosques that do have minarets are often very modest in scale and appearance. Every mosque must have a "quibla" wall so that the prayers of worshippers are properly directed toward the Kaaba in Mecca. They must have facilities for ritual ablution before prayer, and a large enough prayer hall to accommodate all the worshippers. These are religious requirements; there is no obligation to make them aesthetically interesting or attractive. Similarly, some Christians hold firmly to the belief that it is a mistake to regard the "Church" as any sort of building. The true Church is to be found in the community of believers. That is why non-denominational mega-churches are often strikingly functional, with large sums of money more likely to be spent on lighting and sound systems than on interesting architectural features. In Hinduism there is an established difference between the grand palace-style temple which pilgrims visit, and the very modest house-style temple that serves as a simple local shelter for a god.

Still, it remains the case that many religious buildings are to be included among the most spectacular buildings in the world. Some have been treasured and cared for over a very long time. Cambodia's *Angkor Wat*, for instance, is the largest religious building in the world and has been reserved as a place of worship (first Hindu, then Buddhist) since its construction in the early twelfth century. The *Prophet's Mosque* in Medina, one of the largest mosques in the world, is even older, its origins going back to the time of Muhammad himself. Older than either of these is the Church of the Holy Sepulchre in Jerusalem, built in the fourth century on what is believed to be Calvary, the site of the Crucifixion. This ancient church is so treasured that it has literally been fought over by the six branches of the Christian Church that claim property rights with respect to it. Why is it, though, that any religious buildings should be so architecturally outstanding?

The pragmatist aesthetic can help us frame an answer to this question. Consider again the examples of dress and cookery. How we dress, and how we prepare food, are both important components of the aesthetics of everyday life. Simple meals can be exercises in the art of cookery, and inexpensive clothing can be elegant. At the same time, not all dress is everyday dress, and sometimes meals are importantly more than simple. Alongside the everyday are "special" occasions when, as people say, they want to "look their best" and when festive food is prepared. There is an established terminology with which to mark such differences. Dressmaking is to be distinguished from *haute couture* and there is *haute cuisine* as well as cookery. Each of these distinctions constitutes a continuum within the aesthetics of everyday life. Making dresses for very special occasions transforms the "dressmaker" into the "couturier." Preparing food for wedding banquets transforms the "cook" into a "chef." The "art" in question, however, is not confined to the "higher" end. Right across the continuum there is a fusion of the practical and the aesthetic. Bread making is as much an exercise in the art of cookery as the decoration of cakes. What then underlies the difference? The answer is the relative significance of each within the broader context of human life. Weddings, anniversaries, state occasions, are special events. *That* is why they occasion special food and dress. Importantly, the relationship is a dialogical one; part of what makes the event special is that special dress is worn and special food is served.

Precisely the same point can be made with respect to the construction of buildings. In one of his essays Le Corbusier draws a distinction between architecture and "mere building," with the implication that one is an art and the other is not. The same sort of supposition often lies behind the "decorated shed" idea. But however we characterize the distinction, "building" and "architecture" both require a fusion of the practical and the aesthetic. That is why very modest buildings can have aesthetic merits. What distinguishes "architecture" from "mere building" is not the relevance of the aesthetic to the former and its irrelevance to the latter, but the fact that architecture is "special" building in just the way that *haute couture* is special dressmaking.

The "specialness" of architecture is often a reflection of the social importance of the project that the architect is called to undertake. There are relatively few architects whose names resonate sufficiently widely to be ranked alongside the great composers, poets, and painters. One such name, however, is that of Christopher Wren (1632–1723). In the seventeenth century the profession of "architect" did not exist. Wren was a scientist, mechanic, inventor, university professor, and public official who was entrusted with construction projects. In the course of a long career he produced many fine buildings. The most famous of these is St. Paul's Cathedral in London, a new cathedral that replaced the old St. Paul's which was destroyed by the Great Fire of London in 1666. Its completion took thirty-six years, almost the whole of Wren's career as an architect.

The replacement of the Cathedral Church of the Diocese of London was a matter of great public interest. That is why Wren was appointed by a Royal Commission and large sums of money were made available for the work. Immense amounts of time, attention, deliberation, and debate went into the project. Wren did not always have the last word in these debates, and the final result was not entirely in accordance with his wishes. As the long story of the cathedral's construction reveals, at every moment practical and aesthetic debates and decisions were intertwined. What the sometimes intense debate shows is that the project was of great significance not only to the Church of England and to the City of London, but even to the nation as a whole. The construction of this great building was a key element in the restoration of London after a large part of it had been destroyed by fire. It was also an affirmation of London's importance as the nation's capital and an international city of renown. It is easy to see, consequently, why the occasion called for great architecture and not "mere building."

Architecture, then, is special building, just as *haute cuisine* is special cooking. *Haute cuisine* is not to be characterized by the exclusive nature of the cooking methods it uses – boiling, baking, roasting, and stewing are the methods of the everyday as well. Nor is it the exclusiveness of its ingredients – eggs, flour, meat, cream, etc. – though some ingredients will be costly and relatively hard to obtain. The main difference with ordinary cooking is the complexity of its recipes and the skill required in executing them. What results from this is not a different kind of nutrition, but an extra special meal. So too with architecture. Architecture does not have a different product – "work of art" rather than "building." Important differences arise because grand architecture is not fitted to a mundane purpose. That explains the whimsical element in follies. Serious grand architecture requires a socially significant project, which is what Wren's was. Kant was right to single out ecclesiastical, political, and military buildings as categories most likely to call forth architecture. Historically, it is buildings in these categories that have had the right level of social significance to command the services of the greatest architects and give them resources on a sufficiently large scale. This, to return to our starting point, is why such buildings are so prominent in architectural guides.

Art, Architecture, and Religious Buildings

Times change, and one aspect is the changing social significance of things. Kant's categories reflect his own times rather better than they do the architecture of today in at least two respects. First, with the rise and spread of broadly liberal democratic politics (more widely heralded than effectively instituted perhaps), we could drop the category of "palace." No one expects to see contemporary architects building palaces, or devoting their best efforts to royal projects. When occasionally something like this happens – as in the case of the Romanian communist dictator Nicolae Ceaușescu (1918–89), the result is *pastiche*. Political personality cults ape the regal figures of the past, but even if they seem to succeed for a time, the cultural tide has turned against them. In 1977 the infamous Emperor Jean-Bédel Bokassa (1921–96), who took control of what had been French Equatorial Africa, had himself crowned in a ceremony so lavish that it is estimated to have cost $20 million. Extraordinary though this expenditure is, in terms of parity purchasing power it may not be any more than Henry VIII spent on the "Field of the Cloth of Gold," a royal extravaganza in France spread over two weeks in June 1520. The difference that matters is this. Even if by sixteenth century standards this was extravagance, it was the sort of extravagance to be expected in the ruler of a monarchical society. In the twentieth century, Bokassa's extravagance (with his invented regalia) was bizarre enough for political commentators to question his sanity.

A second major change since Kant wrote his third *Critique* is the rise of artistic institutions. As was noted in Chapter 1, it was in the course of the eighteenth and nineteenth centuries that the great capitals of Europe acquired dedicated theaters, concert halls, opera houses, and art museums. These became objects of civic pride, and the buildings that housed them were given the kind of architectural grandeur this implied. Cultural buildings now comprise a further category of outstanding architecture, one that Kant did not list because the emergence of the art world and its newfound social status was only beginning when he wrote. Accordingly, they too appear in the guidebooks. In contrast to palaces, however, it is a category that continues to have the sort of prestige (and perceived importance) that makes buildings of this kind a regular subject of civic commissions and public competitions. Asked to name a famous and exceptional building of the late twentieth century, people whose knowledge of architecture is limited, would probably answer "The Sydney Opera House." Designed by the Danish architect Jørn Utzon (1918–2008), it took fifteen years to complete and cost $16 million (more than twice the original estimate), a sum roughly equivalent to $450 million in 2016. It opened in 1973.

What of Kant's first category, religious buildings? At much the same cost, and taking much the same length of time to construct as the *Sydney Opera House*, the *Mormon Temple* in Washington DC was dedicated just four years later in 1973. Designed by the American architect Keith W. Wilcox (1921–2011), it is a very striking building if not, perhaps, architecturally outstanding. Compared with times past, the construction of a new, architecturally significant and expensive religious building is relatively rare. By contrast, the construction of new, architecturally significant, and expensive cultural buildings is a notable feature of architecture in the late twentieth and early twenty-first centuries. The *Pompidou Center* in Paris (architects Renzo Piano, Richard Rogers, and Gianfranco Franchini) opened in 1977. An imaginative adaptation of the redundant Bankside Power Station in London by architects Jacques Herzog and Pierre de Meuron opened in 2000 as the *Tate Modern* art gallery. Daniel Libeskind's *The Crystal*, an extension to the Royal Toronto Art Museum was completed in in 2001. Zahara Hadid's *Rosenthal Center for the Contemporary Art*s in Cincinnati Ohio opened in 2003. The *Copenhagen Opera House* (architect Henning Larsen), one of the most expensive opera houses ever built, opened in 2005. These are just a few of the best known examples of works by the most highly acclaimed architects. Some are the result of private fundraising and generous donations, but many are civic projects paid for out of public funds.

The contrast with new ecclesiastical building is striking. Though it would not be very difficult to assemble a (limited) list of architecturally significant churches constructed over much the same period, none of them would be projects with such a high profile, and none of them (in the end) would be civic projects paid for by public funds, as Wren's St. Paul's was. Oscar Niemeyer's *Metropolitan Cathedral of Our Lady of Aparecida* in Brasilia is instructive in this regard. This was one of the buildings commissioned by the Brazilian government under the presidency of Juscelino Kubitschek (1902–1976) for the new national capital. The cornerstone was laid in September 1958 and the structure was finished in April 1960. Kubitschek intended the cathedral to be paid for by the state and open to all faiths, but once his presidency ended, subsequent governments ceased to provide funds, and the building was turned over to the Catholic Church to complete. At this point it ceased to be a civic project, and if, arguably, it is now the most famous of the buildings in Brasilia, attracting about one million visitors a year, unlike Niemeyer's *National Congress* (in the same complex), it is not a state building.

Even when public funds are not the issue, it is possible to detect a significant cultural change with respect to religious building. In the first decades of the twentieth century, Princeton University commissioned the architect Ralph Adams Cram (1863–1942), one of the leading figures in the Gothic revival in America, to build a huge university chapel. Its proportions and stained glass are exceptional. The cost (expressed in 2016 prices) was about $26 million. In 2005, the university received a gift from a wealthy graduate worth a little over $100 million for a new arts center. The cultural change over a century that this signifies is reflected in two facts. No one would expect a graduate today to give $26 million for the construction of a chapel and (though this is surmise) the modern secular university would probably not accept such a gift. For such an institution, commissioning a *cultural* building is acceptable whereas commissioning a *religious* building would not be. To this extent, it seems, in the rivalry between art and religion that was discussed in Chapter 1, art has been the winner.

These remarks and comparisons are very broad brush and there is always a danger of over generalizing. The subject of cultural change is complex, and one in which many different factors come into play. In a world that is globally interconnected by wholly new forms of transportation and communication such as the airplane and the internet, cultural evolution is not simply a matter of changing ideas, concepts, and attitudes in an otherwise stable environment. Economic factors are also at work. The decline of Christianity in much of the West has been more than compensated by its rapid growth in Africa and Asia, but these are poor places compared to Europe and America and unlikely to generate the scale of resources required for major architectural commissions. There is also the movement of peoples. In 1998 a large and architecturally striking *Central Mosque* opened in Edinburgh, Scotland, a city notable for the number of fine nineteenth century Christian churches that have closed. The mosque's construction reflects both the presence of a new immigrant population, and the wealth of the Arabic countries that they can call on.

The point of these brief and somewhat speculative observations in this context is as follows. If the pragmatist aesthetic is indeed a solution to the question of architecture as an art, this ties architecture firmly to the shape of social and cultural life, and hence makes it subject to changes within culture and society. Those activities and projects that matter most, and to which people give their principal loyalties, will be the ones that call forth architecture and mark certain buildings out from the general run of construction as truly special. The great palaces of times past that continue to be among the architectural glories of Europe illustrate this. They have lost their original connection with ordinary life. No one could (or could want to) live in the *Palace of Versailles* now, and no one has any reason to make political requests there, as they did in the time of Louis XIV. This means that any continuing interest that Versailles has for the contemporary world must lie elsewhere – as a tourist attraction and a place of purely historic interest. Many historic buildings are in a good structural condition with their architectural features beautifully restored and preserved. Yet in one respect, they are no different from interesting ancient *ruins*, because they have no real function anymore. The social and cultural world in which they did have such a function has receded into the past. Their value, in short, is now only for the world of recreation.

Plainly the same can be true for the temples, abbeys, basilicas, and cathedrals of times past. There is this important difference, of course. Many of them remain in use for worship. It is often the case that these great religious buildings have a dual role. For the millions of visitors who stream through the Gothic cathedrals of Northern Europe and the Baroque churches of Italy and Spain, these too are simply tourist attractions, and sites with historic interest. For a (perhaps diminishing) number of Christians, they are places of worship and pilgrimage that must also accommodate the tourists they attract if they are to secure the financial means to survive. This dual role can even make major new ecclesiastical building possible. Barcelona's extraordinary *Sagrada Familia* basilica was begun by the Catalan architect Antoni Gaudi (1852–1926) in 1882 and has been under continuous construction ever since. From the beginning Gaudi conceived it on a massive scale that would take an age to complete. "My client is not in a hurry" he is reported to have said. On present reckoning it will finally be completed in 2026, the centenary of Gaudi's death. The Pope consecrated the church in 2010 so that its intended purpose is now one of the purposes it actually serves. Its construction, however, has long been funded from an entrance fee charged to visitors, only a small proportion of whom have worshipped in it, or wanted to perhaps.

Sagrada Familia is a remarkable exception to a general trend, not just in the Christian world but in the world of religion as a whole. The Sikh's Golden temple in Amritsar, India (whose official name means "the abode of God"), dates from 1764. It is still a place of worship for upwards to 100,000 people a day, but for all that, it seems very unlikely that such a magnificent construction would be undertaken today. Even more unlikely is a modern equivalent of Angkor Wat, the Cathedral at Aix-la-Chapelle (northern Europe's oldest cathedral) or the Castle Church in Wittenberg where Martin Luther pinned his ninety-five theses to the door.

Our ability to predict the future is notoriously poor, and these surmises can reasonably be questioned. Perhaps there will come a time when the most impressive architectural achievements will once again include religious buildings commissioned as civic and political projects. Who, at the height of the Soviet Union's power, would or could have predicted that by the turn of the twenty-first century, a large number of new churches would be built and opened in Russia? Still, over the last century or more, the civic commissioning of religious buildings has happened only rarely, and as Niemeyer's cathedral in Brasilia shows, when it does happen, it proves temporary.

Churches and mosques, of course, continue to be commissioned. Here, though, there is a further point to be made about the rivalry between art and religion with which this book began, and which connects with some of the themes relating to the visual arts that were discussed in Chapter 3. In that chapter we observed that by abandoning the identifying images of Christianity, modern Western "interpretations" of religious themes – *The Annunciation* was the example explored at length – constitute a rupture with religious art that, by contrast, the art of the icon has preserved. So too, it is possible for religious buildings to be reconceived, as it were, in terms dictated more by the interests of artistic expression than religious identity. Consider this comparison. The Central Mosque in Edinburgh, to return to an earlier example, is the first major Islamic building ever in the city. It was built on land purchased from the City Council, and subject to the planning regulations that govern all buildings in a conservation area of the city. The resulting construction incorporates some elements of characteristically Scottish decorative design, but no one could mistake it for anything but a Muslim mosque. This is because it relies far more obviously on recognizably Islamic motifs – including a very tall minaret.

The ease with which the mosque's Islamic identity registers with even a casual observer contrasts sharply with the parish church of St. Fronleichnam in Aachen, Germany. This is one of the best known buildings of the German modernist architect Rudolf Schwarz (1897–1961). Schwarz contributed several buildings to the reconstruction of Cologne after the destruction of World War II. From the outside, the church he built in Aachen is not recognizable as such. Viewed from some angles, in fact, it would easily be mistaken for some sort of industrial building. It is not hard to identify its modernist style, but this is precisely what disguises its identity as a church. Schwarz's concern with the standards of the art world, in other words, triumphed over the religious identity of the building.

A similar point could be made about many architecturally commissioned churches in the mid and late twentieth century – even about Niemeyer's basilica. Where there has been sufficient money and interest to make it possible, and an architectural competition has been held, the result is almost invariably a building that is more easily identified as a work of modern architecture than a church. Like Magritte's *Annunciation*, there are of course some continuities, since these commissioned buildings must function as churches. Nevertheless, they give us reason to reflect again on one of the issues with which we began – whether art and religion are allies or rivals. Architecture, it seems, in some of its modern manifestations, is evidence of art's ascendancy over religion.

√

6

Rethinking the Sacred Arts

One of philosophy's most important and distinctive tasks is the critical exploration of tacit assumptions. It is characteristic of the philosophical cast of mind that it finds questions to ask and issues to raise that a different cast of mind would be inclined to regard as pointless, and at best a waste of time. That is why people quite often find philosophy's seemingly interminable debates not only worthless, but frustrating.

This response to philosophy is ancient. It receives powerful articulation in some of Plato's dialogues. Socrates's interlocutors often give voice to their irritation and exasperation with his dialectical questions. As Plato appreciates, there is good reason for their reaction. For the most part the activities human beings engage in can only be pursued if certain things are taken for granted. To be constantly questioning the presuppositions on which thought and action proceed is to invite both ignorance and paralysis. Philosophy, Socrates's critics often allege, is a properly valuable educational exercise for young men (they gave no thought to women on this matter), but only *before* the serious business of life begins. Something has gone wrong, accordingly, when a man of Socrates's years persists with it. Life has to be lived, and this means moving on, leaving the student debating club in the philosophical ivory tower to a new generation.

On the other hand – as Plato also sees – from time to time the presuppositions within which we operate distort our ways of thinking and acting. They blind us both to their inherent inadequacies, and to the opportunities that would open up if we were to operate with different presuppositions. There is no denying that it is essential to make some assumptions as we go about our daily business. But what these assumptions are matters. Some will undoubtedly be fundamental truths that no sane person could sensibly deny. Others, though, may only be supposed "truths," propositions, and conceptions that rest on nothing more substantial than unquestioning acceptance, an acceptance that is widespread only because it goes unquestioned. In these circumstances, philosophy can provide the invaluable service of enabling us first to identify what our assumptions are, and then rethinking them.[1]

The purpose of this book has been precisely that. There are some common assumptions, often implicit, about the nature of "art" and its relation to the "sacred arts," which is to say, the relation of religious painting, sacred music, devotional literature, and church architecture to art in general. The aim of Chapter 1 was to identify a view of art that originated with the eighteenth century debates about taste and beauty in which philosophers engaged. There emerged from those debates a view that we might call "aestheticism" which then secured such widespread acceptance among artists, critics, and audiences, that it no longer seemed to need explicit articulation or defense. As a result, it came simply to be taken for granted.

This implicit consensus about art has three dimensions. First it emphasizes art's autonomy. Art, in whatever form, should be pursued and valued exclusively for its own sake. Neither the meaning nor the value of art derives from some extraneous function it serves or beneficial consequence that it has. Second, though art and religion have long been connected, the history of their relationship is best understood as a progressive development in which art gradually secured its autonomy from the service of religion and became a source of inspiration in its own right. Third, this independent source of inspiration derives from a distinctive kind of experience – aesthetic experience. Aesthetic experience is not to be confused with the sort of empirical data on which the acquisition of scientific knowledge rests. Nor is it to be identified with the deliverances of moral sense or mystical encounter. Aesthetic experience is an apprehension of beauty, and something we simply take delight in.

Before long, this hugely influential conception of art led to the creation of social institutions. Art museums, concert halls, theaters, opera houses, schools of art, academies of music grew up as places devoted to

---

[1] The title of this chapter is drawn from a research initiative of the same name undertaken by St. Vladimir's Orthodox Theological Seminary, with the support of the Luce Foundation. I am grateful to Professor Peter Bouteneff, Professor Richard Schneider, and Dcn Evan Freeman for their invitation to participate in a symposium under that initiative in September 2016, and I gladly acknowledge that this concluding chapter owes a lot to our conversations.

and reserved for "the arts." These in their turn then advanced and sustained the conception that gave rise to them. With the consequent development of specialized disciplines such as musicology, art history, and literary criticism, together with the books and journals they generated, there thus came into existence a whole "artworld," one that claimed for itself an exclusive concern with "art proper."

In this way a distinctive, historically contingent conception of art and its relation to life became a settled assumption. In the art world, it is generally supposed, art comes into its own as a distinctive and uniquely valuable reflection of human experience and imagination. Against the background of this supposition, other suppositions follow. Sacred or religious art, for example, has to be understood in one of two ways. The religious music, paintings, sculptures, and buildings that predated the emergence of art proper, can be regarded as *incipient* art – art, certainly, but in a somewhat disguised form and easily interpreted as the promotion or affirmation of religion. Though works like these have religious content, they can still be valued in a highly secularized world that has largely left religion behind. Indeed, such a world ought to treasure them for the non-religious "aesthetic" experience that they can sustain. Religious works, of course, have continued to appear since the emergence of an autonomous art world, but these should now be regarded – like commercial or political art – as belonging to a subdivision of "art proper."

In the case of art's relation to business and politics, there often lurks a suspicion that art runs the risk of subservience to some end other than artistic integrity, that it is easily corrupted into advertising or propaganda. So too in its relationship to religion, where the suspicion is that art has been made subservient to preaching and evangelism. Even among those most strongly committed to the ideal of art's autonomy, however, this danger need not be regarded as grounds for a total embargo on commercial, political, or religious commissions. Artists must live, after all. Still, it does carry the implication that artists freed from any such external service are in a preferable position to those who have to accommodate the interests of "clients."

Chapter 1 argued that what these common suppositions about art in general and the sacred arts in particular ignore, is the extent to which a non-utilitarian concern with appearance, sound, style, touch, and smell permeates almost every aspect of everyday life. These things matter to us no less than nutrition, warmth, and shelter. There is, consequently, an inescapably aesthetic dimension to how we eat and what we wear, to the buildings we construct and the way we decorate them, to the form of our ceremonies, and the content of our entertainment. By denying this aesthetic dimension the status of "art proper," we thus discount a way in which the arts suffuse the things that make us distinctively human – courtship and marriage, home making, cultural festivities, social organization, political engagement, commercial exchange, and religious practice. We can, if we choose, reserve the term "art" for the institutions of the museum, concert hall, literary prize, or poetry festival, and classify the aesthetic dimension of these more mundane activities as "design." But this is a completely unwarranted stipulation that distorts our understanding of the significance of aesthetic judgment and creativity. The aesthetic imagination at its most impressive can be as much in evidence in everyday life as in the more self-conscious art world.

The truth of this contention gives us reason to rethink the sacred arts. If art is not confined to the art world but permeates all forms of human activity, we should see sacred art and its products as neither an artistic legacy from the past nor as "applied" arts in the present. Rather, it is one aspect of the aesthetic imagination at work in a distinguishable context. In this case the context is the everyday life of religious belief and practice.

Along with the assumption that "art proper" is the truest manifestation of art, another important supposition is that painting is the paradigm of the arts. This supposition shows itself in the tendency both artists and critics have had to speak of music as "painting in sound" or literature as "word painting." The effect of this assumption is to further draw the arts away from practical life and see our primary mode of engagement with art as aesthetic "contemplation." But a strictly contemplative attitude is suited – at best – to productive arts, like painting, that result in making an object of some sort. To construe the *productive* arts as a template into which the *performing* arts must be pressed, however, comes at the cost of gross distortion. While we can speak of "painting" in sound or movement, the fact remains that the basic form of engagement with music, drama, and dance is *action*, not contemplation. Passively contemplating art works as viewers in a gallery or as part of the audience in a concert hall is one important mode of engagement with great art, but it is no more central, or valuable, than actively making music, performing a role, or dancing with others.

Questioning and resisting an assumed preference for contemplation over activity is especially important when it comes to rethinking the sacred arts. This is because it is so easily supposed that aesthetic contemplation makes art a natural ally of religion, since contemplation has played an important part in most major religions. To focus on contemplation, however, implies that something like the monastic life is the paradigm of religion, and thus leads us to overlook the role of the arts in both expressing religious emotion and shaping religious ritual. This is especially important when we turn our attention to sacred music. Music is quintessentially a performing art, and to think of musical works primarily as objects of contemplation is importantly mistaken.

On this subject, however, Chapter 2 explored a further danger. The wealth of music that we inherit from the late Classical and Romantic periods has powerfully inclined people to think that music's primary power lies in the expression and communication of emotion. If we think in this way, it seems to follow immediately, that sacred music must be the expression of *religious* emotion. This raises a critical question. However valuable the expression of emotion may be to the person who expresses it, it is hard to see how it could constitute an offering in worship – at least if we think about worship within the framework set by Plato's dialogue *Euthyphro*. Expressing emotion may benefit the worshipper, but how could it benefit the God who is worshipped? Now this difficulty might be averted and the nature of worship better illuminated, if we started thinking of music in some other way. That is why considering some key questions in the philosophy of music is such a valuable preliminary to rethinking sacred music.

In a similar fashion, some widely held presuppositions about the role that representation and resemblance play in visual art can illegitimately constrain our thoughts about the part that paintings, statues, and so on can play in religious life. Once more, our understanding of religious visual art is enlarged if we first engage in a philosophical critique of the underlying assumptions. And in this particular case, the argument of Chapter 3 revealed, while painting and iconography are both visual arts, they differ importantly with respect to their role in religion and its history.

Because of the near universal importance of sacred texts for the religions of the world, literary art must clearly be relevant. Here, however, it seems that questioning presuppositions works the other way around. We are better able to inquire into the status and standing of sacred texts by drawing on some common themes in literary aesthetics. The familiar dichotomy between "fact" and "fiction," for instance, is widely assumed to have implications for Scripture that in other contexts the philosophy of literature has called into question. Reviewing the philosophical arguments can give us the means to break free of the stranglehold that the dichotomy has tended to exercise when we think of the relation of sacred texts to knowledge, belief, and understanding. And, as Chapter 4 demonstrated, attention to other topics in the philosophy of literature – notably narrative understanding and the nature of drama – can prove liberating and illuminating when we try to improve our understanding of the role of a wider range of texts – liturgical and devotional as well as canonical – in religious life.

The widespread assumption that to be true to itself art must be autonomous and free from external constraints of any kind has another crucial implication. It opposes the artistic to the functional, the aesthetic to the useful. Accepting the validity of this opposition, however, raises a seemingly impossible difficulty for any claim that *architecture* is one of the arts. Buildings are essentially functional. They can be beautiful too, but they must have some practical use. To construct a magnificent building entirely for the sake of its magnificence, and without any useful purpose, seems to be the construction of what the eighteenth century rightly called a "folly." Anti-functionalism in aesthetics, then, automatically rules out architecture as an art. This seems especially problematic for religious architecture. Temples, mosques, and churches must figure prominently in any list of the most magnificent buildings in the world. Moreover, for the most part this is no accident. Human beings have repeatedly aimed to make (at least some of) their places of worship aesthetically impressive. At the same time, (with occasional exceptions) the buildings that result are not idle monuments, but spaces with practical uses. How can this tension be resolved? Chapter 5 aimed to address the issue, and to do so by rethinking the sacred art of building places of worship. The key to resolving it, it seems, is not to insist on a radical separation between "architecture" and mere "building," as some architectural theorists have done, but to think of places of worship as lying on a spectrum that can incorporate both humble, yet fittingly attractive, meeting places and spectacularly impressive landmarks.

The opening paragraph of this concluding chapter referred to philosophy's "seemingly interminable" disputes. For the most part, the word "seemingly" is redundant, a temporary concession for the sake of the argument. In reality, most philosophical debates and disagreements are *actually* interminable. That is to say, with a very few minor exceptions, they can never confidently be declared to have come to an end. It is often, and easily, assumed that this makes philosophical debates pointless. Yet that is another assumption we ought to question, and it is called into question by the common retort that sometimes it is more important to journey than to arrive. This familiar reflection, however, is not quite applicable to the case of philosophy. To achieve some measure of philosophical understanding it is essential to arrive at some clearly established conclusions. It is not enough merely to make an honest attempt that nevertheless ends in uncertainty or confusion. What is true, though, is that the importance of arriving at a conclusion does not lie in any new information that has been secured in the process, or in any theory that will now displace all those that went before. The value of philosophical thinking, rather, is more like the value that T. S. Eliot, in one of the greatest religious poems of the twentieth century, attributes to pilgrimage.

> ... the end of all our exploring
> Will be to arrive where we started
> And know the place for the first time[2]

[2] *Four Quartets*, 'Little Gidding' pt. 5

Bibliography

This bibliography includes works cited or mentioned in the texts and additional suggestions for further reading.

Ballantyne, Andrew (2011) "Architecture, Life and Habit", *Journal of Aesthetics and Art Criticism* 69 (1) pp. 43–9.

Barzun, Jacques (1974) *The Use and Abuse of Art*, Princeton, Princeton University Press.

Berger, Karol (2000) *A Theory of Art*, Oxford and New York, Oxford University Press, Inc.

—(2007) *Bach's Cycle, Mozart's Arrow: An Essay on the Origins of Musical Modernity*, Berkeley, Los Angeles, and London, University of California Press.

Bowker, John ed. (1997) *The Oxford Dictionary of World Religions*, Oxford and New York, Oxford University Press.

Brown, David (2004) *God and Enchantment of Place*, Oxford, Oxford University Press.

Butt, John ed. (1997) *The Cambridge Companion to Johann Sebastian Bach*, Cambridge, Cambridge University Press.

Bradley, Fiona (1997) *Surrealism*, London, Tate Gallery Publishing.

Collingwood, R. G. (1938, 1974) *The Principles of Art*, Oxford, Clarendon Press.

Cooke, Deryck (1959) *The Language of Music*, Oxford, Oxford University Press.

Cooper, David (2006) *A Philosophy of Gardens*, Oxford and New York, Oxford University Press.

Danto, Arthur C. (1981) *The Transfiguration of the Commonplace*, Cambridge Mass., Harvard University Press.

—(1995) *After the End of Art: Contemporary Art and the Pale of History*, Princeton, Princeton University Press.

Dawkins, Richard (2006) *The God Delusion*, London, Bantam Press.

Dennett, Daniel (2006) *Breaking the Spell: Religion as a Natural Phenomenon*, New York, Viking.

Gaut, B. and D. McIver eds. (2013) *The Routledge Companion to Aesthetics* 3rd edition, London and New York, Routledge.

Gombrich, E. H. (1995) *The Story of Art* 16th edition, London, Phaidon Press.

Gould, Stephen J. (1999) *Rocks of Ages*, New York, Randon House.

Graham, Gordon (2005) *Philosophy of the Arts: An Introduction to Aesthetics* 3rd edition, London and New York, Routledge.

__(2007) *The Re-enchantment of the World: Art versus Religion*, Oxford, Oxford University Press.

__(2013) "Expressivism: Croce and Collingwood" in *The Routledge Companion to Aesthetics* 3rd edition, Edited by Berys Gaut and Dominic McIver Lopes, London and New York, Routledge.

__(in press) "The Worship of God and the Quest of the Spirit" in *How Shall We Sing the Lord's Song?* Edited by Ben Quash, Vernon White, and Jamie Hawkey, London, Ashgate.

__(in press) "Philosophy, Knowledge and Understanding" in *Making Sense of the World: New Essays in the Philosophy of Understanding*, Edited by Stephen R. Grimm, New York, Oxford University Press.

Guyer, Paul (2011) "Kant and the Philosophy of Architecture", *Journal of Aesthetics and Art Criticism* 69 (1) pp. 7–19.

Hanslick, Eduard (1926, 1986) *On the Musically Beautiful*, Translated by Geoffrey Payzant, Indianapolis, Hackett Publishing Company.

Harries, Karsten (1997) *The Ethical Function of Architecture*, The MIT Press.

Hart, David Bentley (2009) *Atheist Delusions*, New Haven, Yale University Press.

Hegel, G. W. F. (1975) *Hegel's Aesthetics: Lectures on Fine Art* 2 volumes, Translated by T. M. Knox, Oxford, Clarendon Press.

Hess, Barbara and Grosenick Uta (2005) *Abstract Expressionism*, Cologne, Taschen.

Hume, David (1963) "Of Tragedy" and "Of the Standard of Taste" in *Essays Moral, Political and Literary*, World Classics edition, Oxford, Oxford University Press.

Hutcheson, Francis (2004) *An Inquiry into the Original of Our Ideas of Beauty and Virtue*, Edited by W. Leidhold, Indianapolis, Liberty Fund.

Ingold, Tim (2000) *The Perception of the Environment: Essays in Livelihood, Dwelling and Skill*, London and New York, Routledge.

James, William (1902) *The Varieties of Religious Experience*, London, Macmillan.

Kandinsky, Wassily (1977) *Concerning the Spiritual in Art*, Translated by M. T. H. Sadler, New York, Dover Publications. (translation of *Über das Geistige in der Kunst*, 1914)

Kant, Immanuel (1790/1793, 2000) *Critique of the Power of Judgment*, Translated by Paul Guyer and Eric Matthews, Cambridge, Cambridge University Press.

Kieran, Matthew ed. (2005) *Contemporary Debates in Aesthetics and the Philosophy of Art*, Oxford, Blackwell Publishing.

Kivy, Peter (1993) *The Fine Art of Repetition: Essays in the Philosophy of Music*, Cambridge, Cambridge University Press.

Klingsöhr-Leroy, Cathrin (2004) *Surrealism*, Cologne, Taschen.

Leeuw, v.d. Gerardus (2006) *Sacred and Profane Beauty: The Holy in Art*, Translated by David E. Green, Oxford, Oxford University Press.

Le Corbusier (1986) *Towards a New Architecture* 13th edition, Translated by Frederick Etchells, New York, Dover Publications.

Lennox, John C. (2009) *God's Undertaker: Has Science Buried God?* London, Lion Hudson.

Levinson, Jerrold ed. (2003) *The Oxford Handbook of Aesthetics*, Oxford, Oxford University Press.

McGrath, Alister E. (2011) *Why God Won't Go Away*, London, Nelson.

MacCulloch, Diarmaid (2013) *Silence: A Christian History*, London, Allen Lane.

Nagel, Thomas (2012) *Mind and Cosmos*, Oxford and New York, Oxford University Press.

Nietzsche, Friedrich (1878, 2004) *Human, All Too Human*, Translated by Marion Faber and Stephen Lehmann, London, Penguin Books.

—(1883–1886, 2001) *The Gay Science*, Edited by Bernard Williams, Translated by Josefine Nauckhoff, Poems translated by Adrian Del Caro, Cambridge, London, Cambridge University Press.

—(1993) *The Birth of Tragedy Out of the Spirit of Music*, Translated by Shaun Whiteside, Edited by Michael Tanner, London, Penguin Books.

Otto, Rudolf (1923) *The Idea of the Holy*, Translated by J. W. Harvey, Oxford, Oxford University Press.

Pevsner, Nikolaus (1948) *Outlines of European Architecture*, New York, Scribner.

Plantinga, Alvin (2011) *Where the Conflict Really Lies*, Oxford and New York, Oxford University Press.

Plato (1989) *Plato: The Collected Dialogues*, Edited by Edith Hamilton and Huntington Cairns, Princeton, Princeton University Press.

Rookmaaker, H. R. (1970, 1994) *Modern Art and the Death of a Culture*, Wheaton Illinois, Crossway Books.

Ruskin, John, (1959) *The Lamp of Beauty: Writings on Art*, selected and edited by Joan Evans, London, Phaidon Press.

Schleiermacher, Friedrich (1988, 2006) *On Religion: Speeches to its Cultured Despisers*, Edited by Richard Crouter, Press Syndicate of the University of Cambridge.

Schopenhauer, Arthur (1995, 2004) *The World as Will and Idea*, Edited by David Berman, Translated by Jill Berman, London, Everyman.

Scruton, Roger (2004) *Death-Devoted Heart: Sex and the Sacred in Wagner's Tristan and Isolde*, Oxford, Oxford University Press.

Shiner, Larry (2001) *The Invention of Art: A Cultural History*, Chicago, University of Chicago Press.

Stapert, Calvin R. (2000) *My Only Comfort: Death, Deliverance and Discipline in the Music of Bach*, Grand Rapids, Wm B Eerdmans.

Telfer, Elizabeth (1996) *Food for Thought*, London and New York, Routledge.

Venturi, R., D. S. Brown, and S. Izenour (1972) *Learning from Las Vegas*, Cambridge Mass., MIT Press.

Weber, Max (1948, 2004) *From Max Weber: Essays in Sociology*, Edited and Introduction by H. H. Gerth and C. Wright Mills, London, Routledge.

Walzer, Michael (1985) *Exodus and Revolution*, New York, Basic Books.

Wolterstorff, Nicholas (1980, 1996) *Art in Action: Towards a Christian Aesthetic*, Grand Rapids, William B. Eerdmans Publishing Co.

—(2015) *Art Rethought: The Social Practices of Art*, Oxford, Oxford University Press.

Young, Julian (1992) *Nietzsche's Philosophy of Art*, Cambridge, Cambridge University Press.

Index